MW00606996

Cover Illustration: Clambake at the Albert T. Seabury House, c. 1890. LCHS Collection

LITTLE COMPTON
HISTORICAL SOCIETY

Published in the United States by Little Compton Historical Society.

ISBN 978-0-9827069-4-7

First Printing: June 2015

Printed in the United States of America by Sheridan Books, Inc.

Designed by Shelley Bowen.

The Stories
Houses Tell

A COLLECTION OF
LITTLE COMPTON HOUSE HISTORIES

LITTLE COMPTON
HISTORICAL SOCIETY

WILBUR HOUSE

BUILT BEFORE 1690 BY SAMUEL and MARY
(POTTER) WILBUR, FIRST SETTLERS.
HOME OF 8 GENERATIONS OF THEIR
DESCENDANTS

EAST END OF HOUSE 17th CENT., WEST END 18th CENT.
ADDITIONS 19th CENT.

NOW OWNED AND BEING RESTORED BY THE
LITTLE COMPTON HISTORICAL SOCIETY

Today we spell the name and count the generations differently, but the Little Compton Historical Society has been studying the Wilbor House since the 1950s.

ACKNOWLEDGEMENTS

This book is the collaborative effort of a number of researchers, authors, editors, photographers, and designers – the vast majority of whom have volunteered their time to this project.

LITTLE COMPTON
HISTORICAL SOCIETY

Authors are identified at the start of each chapter, and we thank them for the time and care they each took bringing together disparate pieces of information to create the stories that follow. Noted New England House Historian, Marian Pierre-Louis has joined our local authors to provide us with a final chapter providing valuable information on writing house histories.

We are especially grateful to LCHS Board Member Shelley Bowen for her excellent graphic design work and the many hours she volunteered to create this book.

We also acknowledge and thank the contributions made by each of the following:

Research	*Design*	*Review*
Claudia Bell	Shelley Bowen	Jack Angell
Shelley Bowen	Bart Brownell	Claudia Bell
Fred Bridge	Tom Callahan	Bart Brownell
Bart Brownell	Chris O'Toole	Randy Byers
Piper Hawes		Nancy Carignan
Jillian Jennett		Janice Gomez
Marjory O'Toole		Diane MacGregor
Martha Sherman		Carolyn Montgomery
Margaret Webb		Maureen Rego
		Mike Steers
		Caroline Wordell

We are also very grateful for the major financial support provided by the Rhode Island Council for the Humanities for the exhibition and public programs related to this publication.

RHODE ISLAND
COUNCIL *for the* HUMANITIES

The Wilbor House, c. 1690. Painting by Don Cadoret. LCHS Collection.

TABLE OF CONTENTS

Open House, a painting of the Wilbor House Museum. Molly Luce Burroughs, 1963. LCHS Collection.

Introduction

There are in Compton about two hundred houses, which contain, perhaps sixteen hundred persons. Their style of building, like that of their dress and tables is humble and unadorned. They are hospitable to strangers, and friendly in their intercourse with each other; but seem carefully to avoid everything like extravagance in living and refinement in manners.[1]

The Reverend William Emerson, Notes on Compton, 1803

Many of the Little Compton houses viewed by the Reverend Emerson are still standing, and in the two hundred years that have passed since his visit many more have been added to the landscape. Each house holds the stories of the families that have lived there. These stories, or house histories, can be pieced together using deeds, probate documents, photographs, family records and the personal memories of homeowners.

This book contains the histories of nine Little Compton houses, including eight private homes. Their owners generously allowed the Little Compton Historical Society to include the homes in the 2015 Historic House Tour.

Together the house histories tell the story of not just nine buildings or nine families but the wider story of a community as it grew and changed over time. This story includes the first English settlers, summer visitors and Azorean immigrants, and eventually hundreds of soldiers during World War II.

Through the years Little Compton's homes have silently witnessed thousands of lives. Uncovering the stories these houses tell is one important way to better understand and appreciate Little Compton's local history.

We begin with one of the oldest, the Wilbor House.

*The **Wilbor House.** Photo by Bart Brownell.*

The Wilbor House

THE IMPORTANCE OF THE ORDINARY

By Marjory O'Toole

The Wilbor House is perhaps the most studied and best understood historic home in Little Compton, Rhode Island. With the help of a large donation the Little Compton Historical Society purchased the house in 1955 and opened it to the public as Little Compton's first and only museum in 1957. The museum invites visitors into the changing world of an ordinary Little Compton farming family from the late-seventeenth century until the early-twentieth century. As the headquarters for the Little Compton Historical Society the museum welcomes approximately 3,000 visitors each year. Staff and volunteers share the Wilbor House's history with these visitors who include Wilbor family descendants, school children, and historic house and furniture fans.

The establishment of the Wilbor House Museum and the creation of its written history is due in large part to the work of two local historians. The men were thoughtful students of historic houses, thorough researchers of probate and other primary source records, and painstaking genealogists. Their careful study of the house uncovered physical evidence of its changes over time; they thoroughly understood the home's chain of ownership; and they furnished the restored museum based on the probate inventories of its inhabitants. Their work has provided the content for almost all that the Little Compton Historical Society knows about the house and shares with the public.

Even after fifty years the vast majority of that content still rings true. However, during the last fifty years historians and the public have become interested in a wide array of topics that may not have seemed pertinent to local historians working in the 1950s: women's history and property; the lives of the disabled; the roles of servants, immigrants and tenants;

the economics of family businesses; and even wayward children. In recent years some of these topics have made their way into the Wilbor House tour as the Historical Society transitions away from a narrative that focused on antique furnishings and the male heads of households and moves instead toward a narrative that uses the house as an illustration of Little Compton's wider history.

Unfortunately, as new information has been added some old information has been lost. The firsthand knowledge that the founding historians possessed has been clouded by time. Generations of interpreters have passed the information down to their successors, and sometimes misinterpretations have occurred along the way. It is now time for both the clarification and confirmation of old facts as well as the widening of the Wilbor House story to include residents that were underrepresented, ignored, or even unknown in the 1950s. This is possible by revisiting the primary source records, especially the probate records, used by the museum's founding historians. With this new look at an old house the Little Compton Historical Society can now share the story of the Wilbor House and the larger community more accurately and with even greater respect for each of the one hundred men, women and children who lived in the home over the course of 250 years.

WILBOUR & BROWNELL

The men who studied and restored the Wilbor House were both dedicated, life-long, local historians. Benjamin Franklin Wilbour's vocation

was researching local history, especially local genealogy, and most especially the genealogy of his own family, the Wilbors.[1] Upon his death in 1964 he left thousands of pages of typed genealogical and historical notes. Wilbour gave the Little Compton Historical Society a sum of money to publish his town-wide genealogy as well as his notes on Little Compton history. Carlton Brownell took on the role of editor for B.F. Wilbour's work and filled his shoes as Little Compton's unofficial town historian for the next forty years. The two books that resulted from B.F. Wilbour's life's work,

Benjamin Franklin Wilbour.
LCHS Collection.

Little Compton Families and *Notes on Little Compton,* have been the foundation of almost every piece of local history since.

Wilbour and Brownell headed the committee responsible for the restoration of the Wilbor House. Carlton Brownell continued his stewardship of the Wilbor House Museum as Executive Director of the Little Compton Historical Society until his death in 2013. As a young man Brownell undertook an intensive study of local historic houses and was personally responsible for much of the physical work of restoring the Wilbor House. Though he hired professional contractors for the more critical work, Brownell, a practical and frugal man as well as the Head of the History Department at Tiverton High School,

Carlton C. Brownell. LCHS Collection.

would often hire his high school students to do the unskilled labor. The boys would camp out in the Wilbor House during working weekends with sleeping bags and fires in the fireplaces. Brownell later wrote that the boys went through hundreds of gallons of paint stripper to remove 250 years of whitewash from the Wilbor House walls.[2]

Throughout his life Brownell was an admirer of the work of the Society for the Preservation of New England Antiquities (SPNEA now Historic New England). He read their publications and used their buildings as study houses. Perhaps inspired by their policies and procedures, he followed their practice of documenting restorations with photographs. The color slides Brownell took during the restoration of the Wilbor House are an important

High school students restoring the Wilbor House in 1955. LCHS Collection.

tool in understanding the house as it changed through the years. The slides are available in the Little Compton Historical Society (LCHS) online collection and are captioned with notes from a talk Brownell gave in the 1990s.[3] Since Brownell's passing these slides and notes are the best, and in some cases the only, information we have regarding the restoration process.

By using Brownell's slides and notes, genealogies, census records, town records, and the probate inventories of Wilbor House occupants, it is possible to tell a thorough, though certainly not complete, story of one middle class farming family, and by extension gain a better understanding of Little Compton's history. Like the work of Carlton Brownell and B.F. Wilbour, this Wilbor House history will use the chain of male owners to structure the story, but this effort will go further to include as many of their housemates as the sources will allow, to tell a richer more inclusive story of family life and work in early Little Compton.

BEFORE LITTLE COMPTON —
William Wilbor of Portsmouth (c.1630–1710)

William Wilbor of Portsmouth, Rhode Island never lived in Little Compton, but by purchasing farms for four of his sons in what was then pioneer territory, he was responsible for establishing the extensive Wilbor family in the town. Though the name has died out in recent years, according to Carlton Brownell, one fifth of the town's nineteenth-century residents had the last name Wilbor.[4]

When William passed away in 1710 his probate records showed that he owned over 400 £ in cash and bonds as well as land in Swansea and undisposed land in Little Compton, over and above that which he had already given to his children, but William owned almost nothing in the way of moveable property, only his clothing and an iron kettle.[5] With so few belongings and no mention of his homestead in Portsmouth, William, a widower, most likely had already gone through the process of giving away his home and household goods and was living simply with one of his children.

A family genealogy refers to William Wilbor as a "weaver of cloth."[6] Not only did William establish his sons' lives as farmers, he established his son Samuel's second profession as a weaver. From father to son, the craft of weaving passed down to Wilbor House residents as an important source of work, and ultimately income, when they were not consumed with the demands of farming. Evidence of weaving, especially flax, appears in generations of Wilbor family probate documents. The presence of a large loom in the Wilbor House had a major impact on the use of its rooms. The production of cloth provided an important opportunity for the women and even the

Great room restoration 1955. Cloth covers window opening. Marks on floor indicate dividing walls. Photograph by Carlton Brownell. LCHS Collection.

children of the household to contribute to the family income in ways that went beyond daily farming and household chores. Thinking of the Wilbor House as a serious manufactory of cloth as well as a farm is a new and different way to consider the roles of Little Compton's farmhouses and life in early Little Compton.

William, the first of his direct line to settle in America, also established another Wilbor family tradition – that of providing farms for multiple sons.

THE FIRST GENERATION –
Samuel Wilbor (1664–1740) &
Mary Potter (c.1665–Pre-1729)

Samuel Wilbor came to Little Compton as a young man about twenty-five years of age in approximately 1690. His wife Mary Potter was expecting their first child right around that time. Either as a gift or a loan, Samuel's father William made possible the purchase of several lots of land on the east side of the Great Highway (West Main Road) totaling approximately 120 acres. William did the same for three of his other sons, and the four Wilbor brothers established farms all throughout Little Compton. Daniel, a younger brother, was given land in Swansea, and Benjamin, the youngest, may have been given his father's property in Portsmouth.

John Irish's Little Compton stone-ender with additions. Painting by Sydney Burleigh, c. 1900. Courtesy of Jack Nelson.

The Wilbors bought their land from Little Compton's First Proprietors, men from the Duxbury, Massachusetts area, who were granted the right to purchase land from the Sakonnet Indians by King Charles II of England. A majority of the Proprietors had earned the right to purchase land by fulfilling a term of service as an indentured servant. Many moved to Little Compton, but others sold their lots in the last years of the seventeenth century to Aquidneck Island men like Samuel.

Very likely aided by his brothers, Samuel first built a small, one-room structure that later would be referred to as a "porch." He then went on to build the main portion of his home in a style known as a Rhode Island Stone-Ender.[9] The two-story house was nineteen feet square and included an attic. The west wall of the house was built almost entirely of stone and formed a large walk-in fireplace on the first floor and a smaller fireplace on the second floor. Like many early houses Samuel's home faced south. The front door was on the west end of the south wall. According to openings in the walls found during restoration, there were casement windows on the east and south walls. The porch attached to the house on the east wall just north of its casement window. Tight twisting stairs were set behind the south side of the fireplace and led to the second floor and the attic above. Samuel built the nineteen-foot-square portion of the house over a stone foundation that had steps on the north side. The steps still exist and now lead nowhere because of a later addition to the north. Old timers reported to B.F. Wilbour that the Wilbor House cellar was unusable because of ground water flooding, and indeed every spring the basement of the Wilbor House still floods today.[8] However, an eighteenth-century probate document refers to the cellar as usable space.[9] A change in the water table may have occurred over time.

As it appears today the seventeenth-century portion of the Wilbor House is a simple nineteen by nineteen foot square with a single room on the first and second floors and an attic above. The presence of the porch on the east side of the stone-ender was almost lost from memory. B.F. Wilbour and Carlton Brownell believed that it was there from the very beginning and likely predated the main portion of the house as a temporary place to live during construction. The porch and the

Original basement steps during restoration.
Photograph by Carlton Brownell. LCHS Collection.

Porch Chamber above were long gone by the time Wilbour and Brownell studied the house. A letter written by Abby H. Wilbor, the last Wilbor to live in the Wilbor House states, "There was a small porch with one window of diamond panes of glass, moved off when the new porch was added." That would have been sometime between 1850 and 1860 when the old porch was replaced by a slightly larger kitchen addition. Besides probate evidence mentioning the porch and Abby's letter, Brownell found and photographed physical evidence showing the older, lower roofline of the porch below the roofline of the Victorian-era kitchen. He described the porch as probably being constructed in the style of houses at Plymouth with one room on the ground floor and a loft.[10]

Since no visible evidence remains, it is easy for museum visitors to think that the large Wilbor family squeezed into the original two-room house. The presence of the porch changes things in important ways, adding a significant amount of living area for the multiple generations who lived in the Wilbor House. Perhaps the loom was in the porch. Perhaps the boys slept in the loft instead of in the attic as we once thought. In any case the porch provided valuable space for the Wilbor family for almost 200 years.

During the restoration process the committee spent a great deal of time discussing the best way to present the house to visitors. The house had been updated and changed numerous times by the family not only with additions but with new walls dividing old rooms into smaller chambers. This was often done to accommodate the multiple generations living within the home. Ultimately the committee decided to present three different eras that correspond, more or less, to the home's different stages of construction. The first is a late-seventeenth-century era representing Samuel's and Mary's time in the home from 1690 until 1740. This time period is interpreted in the two rooms that comprised the original stone-ender.

Exposed roof-lines of the Victorian-era kitchen and the smaller seventeenth-century porch. Photograph by Carlton Brownell. LCHS Collection.

The second is a Georgian-Federal era that is displayed in five rooms of a large addition added to the north and west of the house around 1740. The third and final time period represents the Victorian era, a time when two kitchen additions were added to the house, one for each family living there. Today the museum displays a Victorian kitchen, a bedroom and hired man's room to interpret this era when the last generation of Wilbor House Wilbors lived in the home.

These choices help visitors understand how the house and daily life on a Little Compton farm changed over time. They are a simplification, though perhaps a necessary one. In order to display these three different time periods the museum founders had to sacrifice the opportunity to show the house with numerous dividing walls and the separate apartments that began to be installed early in the eighteenth century. Physical evidence of these missing walls and apartments is still visible today and helps explain the extent and complexity of changes that took place through the years.

Between 1690 and 1712 Samuel's wife Mary gave birth to eleven children, seven girls and four boys including twin girls born in 1700.[11] Samuel and Mary chose to name their second twin "Thankful" perhaps at the end of a difficult labor or in thanks for a blessing they were not really expecting. This was one of the rare times in the Wilbor House's 250-year history that it would shelter a single nuclear family.

When Samuel's father William passed away in 1710 his will gave some insight into the family's life at that time. Samuel was then a father of ten children and owed his father 43 £, a large sum. William chose to forgive Samuel's debt in his will but in a very grandfatherly gesture instructed Samuel to divide the amount equally between his ten children. In the will Samuel and three of his brothers received portions of his father's "undis-posed" land in Little Compton. This "undisposed" land was over and above the four farms William established for his sons.

Two years later Samuel and Mary's eldest child Martha was the first to leave home when she married James Pearce in March 1712. Her wedding was just a few months before the birth of her baby brother Isaac. Martha's first child would grow up only five months younger than his little Uncle Isaac. The family's generations had overlapped, a not uncom-mon occurrence in Little Compton's large families.

In 1717 Samuel and Mary welcomed a daughter-in-law, Esther Burgess, into their home, and a year later Esther and her husband William welcomed their first child. From that time on the Wilbor House functioned as a home with more than one head-of-household and three or more generations. Each new household created a need for additional space. The addition of William and Esther's growing family likely led to the addition of a northern room that would have given the stone-ender a salt box shape. During the restoration Wilbour and Brownell determined that the northeast corner of the home appeared older than the large 1740 addition. This small north addition may have been added while Samuel and his son William were sharing the house.[12] Dividing walls and additions were added as the growing family needed them. Their exact construction dates remain unclear, but they provided rooms and a degree of privacy for the multiple generations that often lived within the house.

At least ten of Samuel and Mary's eleven children survived to adulthood and were named in their father's will written in 1729/30. Thomas, born in 1704, is not mentioned in the will and neither is wife Mary. Thomas' and Mary's death dates are unknown but their absence from the will is a strong indicator that they had both passed by 1729. Perhaps Mary died around 1729, when she would have been in her early fifties, prompting her husband to write a will he would not need for another ten years. Thomas' brother William named his firstborn son Thomas in 1718, a hint that the elder Thomas had indeed died young. Mary's early death was not unusual for the time. Multiple pregnancies and births, physically demanding work and a lack of quality medical care took their toll on many colonial women.

Samuel's will helps explain the family makeup in 1729/30.[13] At that time Samuel was a widower. He had already given a separate, nearby farm to his eldest son Samuel who married in 1713. Like their sister Martha, Samuel's other daughters Mary, Joanna, Thankful and Elizabeth had married and left home, taking with them sizable gifts of moveable property as was the custom of the time. Daughters Abial and Hannah were unmarried and living at home when their father died. Son Thomas was most likely deceased, and youngest child Isaac was just seventeen years old, still living at home and too young to legally own property of his own. Second son William was thirty-four years old and married to Esther Burgess for twelve years. William, Esther and seven of their eventual twelve children were living with Grandfather Samuel and their aunts and uncle at the Wilbor House which was still likely a two-room stone ender, with a porch to the east, and a one-story addition to the north. Dividing walls in the two nineteen by nineteen foot rooms would have helped provide the household of thirteen with some order and privacy.

Samuel named William his Executor and gave him his dwelling house and the west half of the farm. Isaac was to receive the east half of the farm (which reached to South of Commons Road), but it would stay in his two older brothers' care until Isaac was twenty-one. All profits from that half of the farm were to be for Isaac's use until he came of age. Each half of the farm included about sixty acres, an amount sufficient to support a family. Samuel also gave William and Isaac equal rights to his loom. This bound the young men not just as brothers and neighbors but as partners in the family weaving business. A decade later at the time of Samuel's death in 1740 the loom does not appear in his inventory. Most likely it had already become the property of his sons, or had been re-placed by the younger men with a newer version. Looms and flax appear in probate documents in later generations indicating that the Wilbor House Wilbors were producers of cloth for over one hundred years.

Samuel gave his married daughters each 40 £ in his will, but his unmarried daughters received more — more money as well as moveable property including beds and milk cows that would help ensure their comfort either as married or unmarried women in the future. Each of Samuel's married daughters would have received similar items when they left home.

Samuel's final thought was to create a family burial ground on what was going to be William's property. So that it should, "Reamine for that use and no other forever never to be Sold nor put away that so my family have liberty to bury in it."[14] That cemetery still exists and can be viewed by visitors to the Wilbor House Museum.

Samuel wrote in his will that any unnamed moveable property was to be divided evenly among the children, and any extra money was to be Isaac's. This last line in the 1729/30 will prompted the ten Wilbor siblings and the married daughters' husbands to craft an agreement in 1740 modifying their father's will.[15] They faithfully followed all of his instructions but:

Whereas our Honored father the above said Samuel Wilbour Deceased did make his Last Will and Testament above ten years after he made his, and had gained Considerable in bills of Credit and in bonds for bills of Credit will and was Dessirious upon his Deth bed to make another will to Dispose of what he had gained after he made his said will but had not opportunity: [16]

The siblings and the sons-in-law agreed to divide Samuel's considerable monetary gains more equitably among themselves with Isaac receiving a fair share but no more. The sons-in-law were involved because, as married women, Samuel's daughters could not own property. Everything they had became their husband's property the instant they were wed. Upon their husband's death those items often became theirs once again. Widows and single women were allowed to own personal property and even real estate.

In the last ten years of his life Samuel's estate grew considerably in money, but not in land, or livestock or weaving equipment. This may have been coincidence, or it may have been the conscious decision of a widower to focus on less physically demanding ways of making an income in his later years, a decision to leave the farming and the manufacturing to younger men.

The signatures on the document show that all three of the Wilbor brothers could sign their names, but only two of the seven sisters could do the same. The education of daughters was not a priority for this generation of Wilbors. Most of their neighbors thought in a similar way. A study of the signatures on colonial probate bonds in the Little Compton town vault show that the vast majority of Little Compton men could sign their name well, while the vast majority of women could not.

Shortly after Samuel's death Little Compton's probate officials directed his heirs to have a thorough inventory made of his belongings. The probate inventory would assure a fair division of property between the heirs and would have determined any taxes collected by the town. The inventory makers were neighbors paid by Samuel's estate to do their work. Little Compton inventory makers, and those in other communities, often followed a pattern established by their predecessors, working in a methodical, predictable way starting with the deceased's most personal belongings, usually clothing, then focusing on bedding and the items in their bedroom or sleeping area, then moving through the other spaces in the house, and finally moving outdoors to barns and other outbuildings to record the work-related items in them.

B.F. Wilbour and Carlton Brownell used Samuel's inventory to furnish the seventeenth-century rooms of the Wilbor House. Museum records show that hard-to-find items like spectacles and a looking glass were sought out and purchased in order to honor the contents of the inventory.

Samuel's inventory provides a snapshot of the family home in 1740, but it does not represent every item or even every room in the house. The men taking the inventory included only Samuel's property. Anything belonging to Samuel's children, including the dowry items Esther Burgess brought into the home when she married William, would have been purposely ignored by the inventory takers. Samuel's inventory contents

Spectacles purchased to represent Samuel Wilbor's spectacles. Little Compton provenance. LCHS Collection.

support the idea of the family home as a two-room stone-ender with a porch and possibly a north addition. Samuel's belongings, including a table, chairs, chests, fireplace tools and kitchen items would all have fit well in the Great Room on the first floor. His own bed was very likely in this room as this was a common practice at the time. The chests were full of valuable linens most likely made by members of his own family. The inventory also shows that Samuel was the owner of Abial's and Isaac's beds and bedding. These valuable furnishings, often the most expensive items someone owned, would have gone with them when they moved into their own homes.

Many of Samuel's kitchen items are described as "old" perhaps to distinguish them from Esther's newer items. The family's kitchen items co-mingled on the shared hearth though clearly they were keenly aware of what belonged to whom. After listing kitchen items the inventory moves on to work items including butter and cheese making equipment and flax and wool spinning wheels. These items were most likely in the house but well worth the space they occupied because of the financial benefits they provided the family.

The modest amount of furnishings listed indicate that Samuel's belongings were contained within the first floor of the house leaving the main second-floor room (19 x 19 ft), divided or not, for the use of William, Esther and their growing family. The attic space would also have been available, most likely for a combination of sleeping areas and storage. Samuel's daughter Abial and son Isaac would have also needed space within the crowded house. The porch to the east and its loft were usable spaces. The small north addition was shielded from the stone-ender's fireplace and would have provided a shady, cool room for the production of butter and cheese.

Finally the inventory moves to the barn. Cattle were by far Samuel's most valuable personal property and indicate that their dairying activities were not just for family use but for sale. Newport ships in need of provisions would have provided a ready market. Ferry boats offered an easy connection between Little Compton and Aquidneck Island. Dairy products were an important source of protein in colonial times. Samuel's will ensured that his unmarried daughters would receive milk cows to help provide for their comfortable future.

The wording of the inventory also provides insight into the relationship Samuel and William had as co-heads of household. It specifically mentions Samuel's "right in the corn and grain, and in the live hogs, and in the meat and other provisions" indicating that Samuel and William were truly sharing the farm and the resources it contained, each with his own specific property. William's share of the crops and livestock was his own and would not have been shared with his siblings upon his father's death.

Though it was unusual to do so, Samuel's probate inventory includes his real estate - his Colebrook Road property given to his son Samuel with a value of 800 £ and his homestead farm valued at 2,000 £. By dividing the homestead farm between William and Isaac, Samuel ensured that his three surviving sons received fairly equal portions of the estate. Fairly dividing an estate among one's children is a theme that runs throughout the Wilbor family history and is reflected in the wider community.

B.F. Wilbour and Carlton Brownell believed that the Wilbors were Quakers.[17] There is evidence that certain generations were Quakers, but there is also evidence to the contrary. Samuel appears in a 1732 list of Quakers compiled by the Town Selectmen, but is absent from the 1733 list even though one of his brothers remains.[18] The first several generations of Wilbors used traditional language for dates in their wills, but later generations follow the Quaker custom of avoiding Greek and Roman-based names and using "First Month – Third Day" instead. Samuel's daughter Martha Wilbor Pearce's willingness to own slaves during her married life argues against the first generations of Wilbors being Quakers while their lack of military service argues for it. Fifth generation Clarke Wilbor's obituary states that he was a Quaker but his wife Lurana owned a pew in the Congregational Church.[19] The Wilbors' religious affiliation seemed to change over time perhaps with the ebb and flow of anti-Quaker sentiments in the early years and with marriages later on.

SECOND GENERATION –

Doctor William Wilbor (1695–1774) & Esther Burgess (1696–1760)

Samuel's second son William married Esther Burgess on June 20, 1717. He was twenty-two and she was twenty-one. Between 1718 and 1742 Esther bore twelve children. Two of their daughters, Esther and Lydia, died young and their names were given to sisters who were born a decade later. Esther was forty-five when she had her last child Clarke, who did not survive to adulthood. His birth was recorded but his death date is unknown.

Four years before his own marriage William watched his brother Samuel marry. Samuel Senior gave Samuel the Second a nearby farm of his own. We do not know if the younger Samuel and his bride ever lived in the Wilbor House. William and Esther did move into the family home and spent the rest of their lives there. The giving of separate farms to older sons and the inheritance of the family home by a younger son is repeated throughout 250 years of Wilbor House history. It shows that the Wilbor family home was not seen as a privilege for the first born but was more of a consolation prize for later-born sons. Inheriting the family home often came with strings attached. More than once, unmarried aunts, uncles or siblings were given a life-long right to live in the house. Wills enabled deceased fathers to direct their sons from beyond the grave requiring them to care for these relatives indefinitely. The house was often a safe haven for relatives who could not care for themselves and a lifelong responsibility for the younger sons who inherited the property.

This custom of leaving a family home to a younger son was common not just for the Wilbors but throughout New England.[20] It differed greatly from the English law of primogeniture in which the eldest male heir automatically inherited the estate. The ability for New England's younger sons to so easily become yeoman or land owners helped shape a new way of life and a new economy in the colonies that made upward mobility and a middle-class lifestyle far more attainable in America than in England.[21] Following this new American custom, second son William became the Wilbor House patriarch and in effect family patriarch as well.

Though there is nothing in the family's probate documents to confirm that William was in fact a doctor, B.F. Wilbour states that he was a "Doctor of Physic" in *Little Compton Families*.[22] Town council records refer extensively to a "Doctor William Wilbour" during an epidemic in 1757, but there were five other William Wilbors living in Little Compton at that time who were appropriately aged to be a physician. How could B.F. Wilbour be so sure when family documents never refer to this William as a doctor? At the time of his death, William's father Samuel owned only a Bible and one other book. When William died it was the same, a Bible and another book listed among his belongings. There were no medical books or medical equipment listed, providing no evidence that William grew up in a household that would have encouraged him to study medicine, or that he ran a household that functioned as a medical office.[23] B.F. Wilbour seldom cited his sources. He may have had access to something that confirmed William's role as a physician beyond any doubt, he may have been using family history, or he may simply have deduced the answer. Some compelling bits of evidence that this William was indeed a doctor are that his eldest son Thomas became one as well, and that William owned a horse. We will trust in B.F. Wilbour's conclusions and assume this William was in fact a physician.

William's role as a doctor opens a new chapter in the story of the Wilbor House expanding its use as a multi-generational home, a farm office, and a manufactory of cloth, into a part-time hospital as well. In at least one case it is clear that Doctor William brought a patient to recover at his home. This would have made patient care not only his responsibility but also his wife's and perhaps his daughters'.

In the early spring of 1757 a terrible epidemic moved through Little Compton's Native American population. Town council records show that the town paid for at least five coffins and winding sheets in order to bury the dead.[24] The records also show that Doctor William Wilbor was deeply involved in the care of the sick especially Fallee Solomon.[25] Fallee, who was described as an "indeon girl," was left orphaned by the epidemic.[26] William brought her into the Wilbor family home for care and possibly for medical treatment. After one year of care the town paid him 60 £ for his trouble, but at that point the town decided they would pay no more. The selectmen voted instead to indenture Fallee to Doctor Wilbor until her eighteenth birthday. She would work for the Wilbor family in return for food and shelter. When she left the family they would have likely provided her with a new set of clothing and a Bible as was the custom with most local indentures.[27] Unlike voluntary indentures which were negotiated between a child's family and his or her future employer, Fallee was the subject of a forced indenture, arranged and monitored by the town in order to prevent her from becoming "chargable" (a financial burden) to the town. The arrangement may have been beneficial to Fallee, but beneficial or not, she had no choice. Fallee became the Wilbor's servant and the only known Native American to live in the Wilbor House.

Where would Fallee have stayed within the house? By the time she arrived in 1757 the building was very different than during Samuel Wilbor's lifetime. It would have included a small kitchen bedroom that would function very well as a sick room. Once she was well, the kitchen itself, the porch loft, the attic or an "open chamber" over the kitchen could have been used as a sleeping area for an indentured servant girl. According to Carlton Brownell many local homes had a roughly-finished, unplastered room upstairs over a rear kitchen that was called an "open chamber." The room was used for storage and for housing servants.[28] Each of the possible servants' quarters was less desirable than the bed chambers used by family members though the kitchen at least would have been warm. A 1774 newspaper article reported that a "Negro" woman belonging to a Newport family froze to death in her unheated bed chamber.[29]

EXPANSION

Sometime between Samuel's death in 1740 and Doctor William's death in 1774, the Wilbor House more than doubled in size. No specific date is known, but based on architectural details, Carlton Brownell concluded the change took place close to 1740 when both Doctor William's and his son William the Second's families were living there. Shortly after Samuel's death the home was occupied by his unmarried daughter Abial, Doctor William, Esther and nine of their ten surviving children. Eight years later in 1748 William the Second married and started his own family of ten children. This period between Samuel's death in 1740 and William the Second's marriage in 1748 is a very logical time for expansion as the already-full house anticipated the arrival of a new daughter-in-law and another generation.

There is no real evidence of expansion in Doctor William's 1774 probate records. The doctor was a widower by this time and his belongings were simple and few. William the Second's 1796 will and inventory clearly refer to the new addition to the house. Architectural details remain the best evidence of the expansion date. In addition to Carlton Brownell's conclusions, architectural historians including Lombard Pozzi and Mack Woodward have visited the house and agree with a mid-eighteenth century date for the expansion.

At this time the Wilbors transformed their home from a seventeenth-century stone-ender into an imperfect Georgian-style Colonial. They took down most of the stone-ender chimney and fireplace and replaced them with three brick fireplaces on the ground floor and two on the second floor all connected to a large center chimney. The kitchen fireplace to the north has a bee-hive oven. Archaeologist Kate Johnson discovered that the masons threw many of the chimney stones into the yard creating a patio-like surface to the south that is now several inches under the grass.[30] A number of large stones were used in the chimney in the attic, perhaps in an effort to save bricks or to avoid moving particularly heavy stones, creating an interesting mix of building materials. The family added a two-story addition to the west equal in size to the original stone-ender with a large sitting room and two large bed chambers above. They enlarged the front hall

Expanded Wilbor House. Engraving by Richard Kinnicut, 1936. LCHS Collection.

and stairs (though they remained cramped), expanded the north addition to match the new length of the house to create a new "long kitchen" complete with a kitchen bedroom and pantry downstairs and an open chamber upstairs and, finally, raised the attic roof to accommodate the additions. They replaced casement windows with sash windows, and the former Great Room, now with its new smaller brick fireplace, was divided (or continued to be divided) into three smaller rooms. Differences in whitewash patterns on the ceiling and faint marks on the floor indicate where some of the dividing walls were placed. The old porch to the east remained.

In its expanded form the Wilbor House had the basic appearance of an eighteenth-century Georgian-style home. Close observation reveals that the second-story windows on the eastern, older part of the house are not perfectly aligned with the second floor windows in the newer, western part of the house. A seventeenth-century beam was in the way and prevented a perfect Georgian symmetry on the home's façade.[31] Brownell also believed that the original windows in the back of the expanded house were smaller than those in the front, a cost saving measure.[32]

Already a widower for twelve years, Doctor William Wilbor wrote his will in 1772 two years before his death.[33] In it he mentions his oldest son Doctor Thomas Wilbor, the first Wilbor House resident to have moved out of Little Compton. William's language indicates that he has already provided for Thomas in some major way and now leaves him a token amount. The doctor handles his daughters in a similar way mentioning each daughter's name then "what I have already Given her," and giving one silver dollar more. His daughter Lydia the Second had already passed by 1722 and her two daughters were given significantly more, one hundred silver dollars each when they turned eighteen. Though there is no way to know for sure, this bequest to his granddaughters indicates that each of his surviving daughters had already been given cash or moveable property equal to about 200 silver dollars.

To three of his sons Doctor William leaves the farms and homes in which they and their families were already living. The doctor had allowed them to live there earlier, perhaps much earlier, but did not make their ownership official until his death. This was common in colonial times and helped ensure a son's loyalty to his father in hope of a reward at his death.[34] William the Second, the doctor's third-born son, officially received the family farm on which he had been living with his own family since 1748. Why did William the Second receive the family farm and not the others? It may have been by default.

William the Second, age twenty-one, married seventeen-year-old Hannah Wilbor, a distant cousin, in September 1748. Their first child Mary was born in February just five months later. Faced with a premarital pregnancy William and Hannah's options were limited. A quick wedding was the only solution that protected Hannah from questioning and possible punishment from the town council. Living with William's parents was also very likely their best option for a home. William and Hannah's situation was not uncommon. In her book *A Midwife's Tale*, Laurel Thatcher Ulrich notes that thirty-eight percent of the 816 babies delivered in Maine by midwife Martha Ballard between 1785 and 1812 were conceived out of wedlock.[35]

We may never know if Doctor William and Esther Wilbor accepted their pregnant daughter-in-law with warmth and understanding or with judgment and scorn, but in either case it was Doctor William's choice to offer the younger William a place at the homestead farm and not a farm of his own. Perhaps it was the simplest and best way to help the young couple with their new family. Perhaps it was a penance for bad behavior. Without more evidence, it is impossible to tell. By 1772 Doctor William thought highly enough of William the Second to name him executor of his will and to leave him everything else that he had not otherwise given away. Once again a younger son became the Wilbor House patriarch and took on a leadership role in the family.

The highlights of Doctor William's inventory include forty-one and a half pounds of flax, a clear sign that linen production was important to the family; a looking glass, silver spoons, and knives and forks, indicating a certain degree of refinement, and a very unusual mention of gold money. The doctor owned farming tools but no livestock (with the exception of a mare that he could have used to visit patients) showing that he had given up farm work by the age of seventy-nine.[36]

THE THIRD GENERATION —
William Wilbor, The Second (1727–1796) &
Hannah Wilbor (1731–1822)

On the eve of the Revolution in 1775 the Wilbor House would have included William the Second age 48, his wife Hannah (44), their unmarried adult daughters Mary (26), Lois (23), Esther (21), their first-born son Joseph (18), William (15), Jonathan (13), Deborah (11), Embling (also Emlin, 8), Benjamin (6) who may have been disabled from birth and Hannah (5). This is the first time since 1718 that the house may have only contained a single nuclear family. William and Hannah's family is remarkable in that six of their ten children, Benjamin and five daughters, remained unmarried and lived their entire lives within the Wilbor House ensuring the multigenerational use of the building until Lois' death in 1844 at the age of ninety-two.

Lois, Mary, Deborah, Embling and Hannah the Second were true "spinsters," unmarried women occupied in the family's work of cloth production. At their father's death his inventory showed that he owned ninety-one yards of various types of new cloth, eighty skeins of linen and tow yarn, and six skeins of wool yarn with a value of $41. The Wilbor men may have been called "weavers," but all of these valuable market goods were made at least in part through the labor of the Wilbor women. Hannah was the first Wilbor House wife to outlive her husband and was viewed by the federal census taker of 1810 as the head of her own household of six adult women. Her son Jonathan's household of nine shared the Wilbor House with her.[37]

William the Second's 1796 will took great pains to care for his wife, five unmarried daughters and disabled adult son by providing them with lifetime residency in the Wilbor House and requiring that his two younger sons William (Judge William) and Jonathan provide for them equally.[38] Though Hannah and her daughters were undoubtedly contributing work to the household, the perpetual care of seven individuals was a major responsibility. William the Second was being both fair and practical by dividing that responsibility between two able-bodied men. If one should fail for any reason, the other could carry on. William the Second's oldest son Joseph had already received his own farm and was given no responsibility for the care of his mother or unmarried siblings, another example of differing treatment and expectations for first-born and younger sons.

Unlike his father's and grandfather's probate documents, William the Second's will used very precise language describing the Wilbor House and gives us a clear idea of the house's expanded structure in 1796. William the Second did not specify which parts of the house his sons Judge William and Jonathan or even Benjamin would occupy, but he went into great detail regarding rooms for his wife and daughters. As long as Hannah remained his widow she received "the use and improvement" of the west half (the newer half) of his home upstairs and down except the southwest chamber bedroom (with a fireplace) which he assigned to his daughters. Hannah's rooms would have included a southwest sitting room with a fireplace, a portion of the new kitchen, the kitchen bedroom, the pantry, and the northwest bedchamber. If she remarried she was expected to move out.

Benjamin was provided for as follows:

As my son Benjamin Wilbour is not likely ever to be capable to
conduct for hiself therefore I do hereby give him a comfortable deasent
maintainance of all Necessaries of Life both in sickness and in health
and at all times during his natural life to be provided performed and
done by my two sons Namely William and Jonathan or their legal
representatives equally divided between them.[39]

Benjamin disappears from the historic record after this mention. He is not listed as part of his mother's household in 1810.[40] It is likely he did not live as long as his mother or sisters and never accumulated any significant personal property. Benjamin's story, though short on details, is a reminder that Little Compton's population has always included people with disabilities and provides some insight into the care their families provided.

The Southwest Bed Chamber as it was interpreted in 1970. LCHS Collection

The wording of William the Second's will leaves open the possibility that Judge William lived in the Wilbor House at least for a time. In fact the 1810 census lists a William Wilbour in between Jonathan and Hannah, but since Little Compton's houses did not have house numbers, it is difficult to say for sure. According to B.F. Wilbour, Judge William lived across the street on family land that extended west to the Sakonnet River.[41] The area of land owned by Samuel Wilbor's descendants was huge at this time, reaching from the Sakonnet River to South of Commons Road and from north of Taylor's Lane to Swamp Road. For generations the Wilbor House patriarchs had been successful in accumulating enough land during their lifetime to provide for all their sons.

Jonathan and his household lived on the older, eastern side of the Wilbor House. The presence of Jonathan's mother and unmarried siblings would impact his use of the home, and dictate the tasks that must be performed and the provisions provided, not only during his lifetime but also during that of his son Clarke. During his widow Hannah's lifetime, William the Second's will required their sons William and Jonathan (and later Clarke) to consistently provide two cows and a horse for their mother and:

> *To provide and deliver for her [the widow Hannah] each & every year 15 bushels of Indian Corn and five of Barley half a hundred of Flower Quarter of a hundred of shugar and five gallons of Molassas: Also Two hundred weight of Pork Two hundred weight of Beef and a sufficiency of Sutable sauce for the same and one Bushel of good salt and six cord of fire wood delivered to the door a sutable length for the fire also fourty weight of good flax and twenty weight of good sheepswool during her widowhood.[42]*

William the Second also dictated that after Hannah's death William and Jonathan provide the same supplies, with the quantities adjusted downward, to their sisters as long as two of the unmarried women remained in the house. If his last wishes were followed, these provisions and tasks would have continued for forty-eight years amounting to an enormous financial responsibility. This was the price that Judge William, Jonathan and Clarke were required to pay for the privilege of inheriting the family home. In this particular case the responsibility was so great, it again raises the question of whether inheriting the Wilbor House was a privilege or a penance.

THE FOURTH GENERATION —

Judge William Wilbor (1760–1843) &
First, Mary Southworth (1757–Pre-1833) &
Second, Deborah Chase (1788–1866)
Jonathan Wilbor (1762–1822) &
First, Esther Woodworth (1759–1789) &
Second, Priscilla Wilbor (1774–1838)
Mary Wilbor (1749–after 1813/before 1825)
Lois Wilbor (1752–1844)
Embling Wilbor (1767–1825)
Hannah Wilbor (1770–1825)
Benjamin Wilbor (1769–After 1796/Before 1810)

Judge William Wilbor's home across the street from the Wilbor House was called Onegan. Through the years it has been expanded into the Brayton family home. In 1787 Judge William married Mary Southworth. The couple had one child named Andrew, but the boy died very young. Neither Andrew's nor Mary's death dates are known. Many years later in 1833 at the age of sixty-three William married forty-five-year-old Deborah Chase. Deborah became his widow in 1843 and lived another thirty-three years at Onegan. William was the first owner of the Wilbor House to die without children, a foreshadowing of things to come when two generations later the lack of children ended the Wilbors' 250-year residency in the home.

William outlived his brother Jonathan by more than twenty years and remembered Jonathan's widow and children generously in his will. Despite, or perhaps because of, the closeness in which they lived and worked, and the responsibilities they had for each other, the Wilbor family members seemed to have maintained good relationships. The respect and courtesy shown to each other in this and in previous generations of family wills bear witness to the trusting relationships family members must have shared.

Like William, Jonathan also married twice, but both times were in his youth. His first wife Esther Woodworth died in 1789 just two years after they were married, most likely due to complications following the birth of their daughter Esther. This young mother's death is a reminder that medical treatment was still crude at the end of the eighteenth century, and that childbearing women were at risk. Two and a half years later Jonathan married a distant cousin, Priscilla Wilbor, and the couple had six more children.

Jonathan's unexpected death in 1822 at the age of sixty must have greatly upset life on the Wilbor farm not only for his wife and children but for his siblings as well. Jonathan had not been preparing for death. He left no will, and he died in debt.[43] Judge William and Jonathan's twenty-six-year-old son Clarke were now responsible for the farm and the care of at least three unmarried relatives.

The unexpected timing of Jonathan's death provides a window into the daily workings of his 1822 farm. The probate inventory prepared by two of his neighbors shortly after his death reflects the belongings of an active man still working hard to support his wife and dependent children. In contrast the probate inventories of his father, grandfather and great-grandfather were all written late in life representing lives of semi- or full retirement with little or no livestock and devoid of the farming implements and household items that had already been given to adult children.

Probate officials appointed Judge William as Jonathan's executor and ordered him to sell Jonathan's personal property in order to pay his debts. As the widow and new head-of-household for a family of four (herself, daughter Judith (24), son William (22) and son Jonathan (18)), Priscilla requested an "allowance" and was permitted to prepare a list of necessities that would be exempt from sale. This list was akin to a widow's right to a third of her husband's estate. The probate officials approved her list without argument. The difference between the full inventory of Jonathan's belongings and Priscilla's list of required goods helps us understand the difference between the essentials of daily life in 1822 and the extras that both Priscilla and local probate officials agreed could be sold.[44]

Jonathan's list of belongings shows that in 1822 the Wilbor House was not only a farm and a manufactory of cloth but also a shoemaker's shop. Son Jonathan Junior carried on that trade. The Wilbors were still growing flax and corn but had added potatoes, red beans and hay to the mix. Livestock included three hogs, five geese, twenty-one fowls, two turkeys, seventeen sheep, four cows, two oxen and a horse. A very large supply of pork and beef had been set by.

As her allowance, Priscilla kept four out of seven beds, two out of eight spinning wheels, one half to one third of the linens and almost all the furniture including the best chairs and the second best runlet (small barrel). She kept only the Bible from among the books, only four hens and one cow from the livestock, a small portion of the preserved meat and grains, half of the flax, one half to one third of the kitchen wares and all of the silver spoons. New cloth, the extra beds, livestock, meat and crops were the most valuable items to be sold. The probate officials did not assign a value to the food items kept by the family as they were basic necessities and not assets. Pricilla's list of necessities amounted to just over $200 of the $900 inventory. There was no accounting of the sale of items or the payment of debts, but Judge William would have followed through on those responsibilities and kept a watchful eye on his brother's family especially his nephew Clarke who was now his partner in the family farm.

Shortly after her husband's death Priscilla's father also passed away leaving her $500 in cash and several valuable household items.[45] This inheritance helped pave the way for more stable finances in the next generation led by Priscilla's son Clarke, whom she had named after her father.

Judge William's and Jonathan's dual inheritance of the Wilbor farm is an example of the growth and division that the farm experienced generation after generation. Each head of household worked to accumulate real estate in the immediate area and then divided it among his heirs. Tracking the changes in acreage over time would be an enormous job and has not yet been done, but we do know that the original Samuel Wilbor farm consisted of two fifty-acre lots and two eleven-acre lots acquired from the town's First Proprietors.[46] The combined 122 acres stretched between West Main Road and South of the Commons. Through the generations Samuel's heirs acquired and then bequeathed nearby farms in a much larger area stretching from the Sakonnet River to South of the Commons and from Swamp Road to north of Taylor's lane. At his death the childless Judge William gave his farm on the east side of West Main Road "back" to the family patriarch Clarke reuniting the Wilbor House's divided acreage and rebuilding the family holdings to benefit future generations.

THE SPINSTER SISTERS

As mentioned above, William the Second provided for his five unmarried daughters, Mary, Lois, Deborah, Embling and Hannah, with lifelong residency in the Wilbor House. They lived as a household under their mother's care until her death in 1822 just three months before their brother Jonathan's death. The sisters' probate documents are the best information available regarding their lives and roles within the family.

Mother Hannah endured the death of one unmarried daughter, Deborah, age forty-nine, in 1813. The wording of Deborah's will indicates that like her father, William the Second, she was a Quaker. She left her belongings to her sisters and her money to Jonathan's children. The rest and residue went to her brother William. Deborah left nothing to her disabled brother Benjamin, another indication that he had died by this time.[47] Though there is no documentation, it is possible that Deborah moved from the Wilbor House across the street to Judge William's much less crowded home, Onegan, to serve as his housekeeper after the death of his first wife. Her bequest to William and her use of the term "who live with him" when referring to Jonathan's children hint that she might have lived in a different house.

Very little is known about Mary. She appears not to have made a will nor to have had her property inventoried. Even her death date is unknown. Her sister Deborah mentioned her in an 1813 will, but her sister Hannah does not in 1825. Mary likely passed away sometime during that eleven year period. Mary is not listed in the Little Compton Cemetery index completed by B.F. Wilbour in 1937. If, like her sisters, Mary was a practicing Quaker she may have been buried with an uninscribed stone in the cemetery in back of the Friends Meeting House or in the family plot.

Sisters Hannah and Embling died just eight days apart in April of 1825 at the relatively young ages of fifty-five and fifty-eight respectively. Embling did not write a will. Hannah wrote hers the day after Embling died.[48] Why would two middle-aged sisters die a week apart from each other? The women may have succumbed to a contagious illness, or they may have been injured in an accident, even a fire. Photographs taken during the restoration of the Wilbor House show that there was a fire in the northwest bedroom, a room assigned to their mother Hannah. As more and more historic newspapers are digitized we may one day be able to uncover the reason for the sisters' deaths.

Embling's probate inventory indicates that she owned one bed and a large quantity of linens including twenty-four sheets. The rooms she shared with her sisters would have contained her clothing and her furniture: two chests, and a box, a looking glass, three chairs, a table, candlesticks, her books and her fireplace tools. Her father had given her the right to store items in the garrett or attic which she did, and there she may have kept her baskets and meat tubs and yarn. She also had a right to use the kitchen and owned a variety of wooden, pewter and iron ware, glassware, knives and forks, coarse earthenware dishes and a much finer set of porcelain "Liverpool ware." Her valuables included cash notes amounting to over $450 and $43 in old silver.[49] If Embling was injured in a fire, it was not extensive enough to destroy her belongings.

A scorched wall in the Northwest Chamber indicates a fire. The Open Chamber is visible through the doorway. Photograph by Carlton Brownell. LCHS Collection.

All the above items were Embling's and Embling's alone. Had she married they would have instantly become her husband's property, but as a single woman she was allowed to own them and do with them as she wished. She may have received these items as gifts from family members, bequests from her father, mother, and sisters Deborah and Mary. She may also have earned them either by making them herself or by trading or selling her work, most likely spinning and weaving, to attain them. If each of Embling's sisters had similar items, as they likely did, then the western half of the Wilbor House was certainly a well-furnished home.

During their lifetimes, in addition to accumulating personal property, Hannah, Embling and Lois did something rather remarkable for Wilbor women; they acquired real estate. Even though they were land owners themselves, the sisters chose not to give their land to female relatives, at least not permanently. Hannah left her sister Lois the use of her real estate during her lifetime but willed it to her nephew Clarke after Lois' death. Lois purchased Embling's real estate from her executor and willed that portion of the land to Clarke as well. Thus Hannah and Lois followed the family custom of returning land to the head of the Wilbor House for the use of future generations.[50]

Lois survived all of her unmarried siblings by almost twenty years. She wrote her will twenty years before her death in September of 1825. Perhaps she had the same illness that took the lives of Hannah and Embling and feared she would not survive. Perhaps she was reacting to losing two sisters so close together, or perhaps she wanted to avoid the confusion that Embling's intestate estate may have caused. Lois, too, followed the Quaker custom of using numbers to indicate months and days rather than using the Greek and Roman terms in her will.

Lois' long life raises some interesting questions. What were her brother Judge William's and her nephew Clarke's obligations to her after her sisters' deaths in 1825? Her father's will stipulated that his daughters were to be provided with food and firewood as long as *two* of them remained unmarried. Now that Lois was the last unmarried daughter was she responsible for her own provisions, or did William and Clarke continue to provide for her? Whatever the arrangements, they must have been friendly as Lois chose Clarke to be her executor. Lois' father had given her the use of upstairs rooms. This arrangement may have become impractical or even impossible as Lois moved into her eighties and nineties. Again, Lois' choosing of Clarke to handle her estate and the bequests made in her will indicate that she was content with the care the family gave her. Lois' probate inventory was not detailed, but at her death she owned a tract of land, $25 in clothing, $75 in furnishings and a comfortable $1,800 in cash and securities.[51]

Over the course of her lifetime Lois lived with five out of the six generations of Wilbors to live within the Wilbor House. She lived under the watchful eye of four patriarchs: her grandfather Doctor William, her father William the Second, her brother Jonathan, and her nephew Clarke, and she witnessed the birth of the home's final family members her grand-nephews William and Oliver.

THE FIFTH GENERATION —

Clarke Wilbor (1796–1855) &
   Lurana Taylor (1800–1860)

Clarke Wilbor was the first, first-born son to inherit the Wilbor House. Why the change in tradition after 200 years of first-born sons being given their own farms and later-born sons inheriting the homestead? Clarke may have made that change a necessity by following in the footsteps of his grandparents and conceiving a child before marriage. In November 1817 at the age of twenty-one Clarke married seventeen-year-old Lurana Taylor. The couple had their first child six and a half months later. Clarke's youth, the urgency of the situation, and his father Jonathan's uncertain finances may have made moving into the Wilbor House the best, or even the only, option for Clarke and his young bride.[52] Clarke worked as a schoolmaster at the nearby Peaked Top School to help make ends meet.[53] He and Lurana had nine children between 1818 and 1840.

When Clarke's father passed away in 1822, Clarke was twenty-six years old and shared the older, eastern portion of the Wilbor House with his wife Lurana and the first three of their children as well as his mother Priscilla, his younger sister Judith and two younger brothers William and Jonathan. His Grandmother Hannah's death in January 1822 ended her occupation of the rooms in the newer, west addition of the home and provided badly needed space for the younger generations. However, at least one upper room to the west was still occupied by Aunts Lois, Embling and Hannah. The inhabitants and the purposes of each room in the Wilbor House must have changed regularly as the family grew and changed, but at this time four generations found a way to live together under one roof in a home that was for all intents and purposes functioning as a tenement apartment building.

Peaked Top School. Painting by George Burleigh. LCHS Collection.

As its patriarch, Clarke added to the Wilbor House assets by building
(or purchasing) a windmill on West Main Road on what is now the site
of the New Wilbour Cemetery.[54] He added a "Waggon-House" or
carriage house to protect the family's multiple vehicles and was able to
purchase several new wood lots to add to the family holdings.[55]

The 1850 Federal Census was the first to list each member of a household
by name and provides valuable information regarding Clarke and Lurana's
home. Their second son Alexander and his new bride Abbie Catherine
Gray were living in the Wilbor House at the time. Alexander was a
carpenter while his younger brothers William and Oliver were laborers
on their father's farm. Oliver at age nineteen and his younger brothers
were still attending school.[56] It often took students many years to finish
the eight grades the local schools offered. Teachers knew that farm work
had to come first and were very flexible with their students' attendance.

Abbie Catherine became much better known in later years as local
midwife Aunt Kate Wilbor.[57] Alexander and Kate's stay in the family

home, no matter how short it may have been, is important because it shows that even sons who would one day be given (or who would purchase) a farm of their own may have lived as newlyweds with their parents. In this case, too, the Wilbor House served as a safe place to roost for family members who could not make it on their own, at least not yet. Alexander and Kate eventually moved into their own home just south of Clarke and Lurana.

Clarke, who must have been ill at the time, wrote his will in September of 1855 at the age of fifty-nine and died in December of the same year. Like his father, Clarke died a relatively young man still actively farming and providing for his family. Like his grandfather, he made provisions for his wife and unmarried daughter Deborah to live comfortably at the Wilbor House for the rest of their unmarried lives. Clarke structured those provisions very much like his grandfather did, assigning Lurana and Deborah specific rooms, including the Southwest Chamber once assigned to his aunts, and dividing the farm and its responsibilities between two sons, requiring them to share in their mother's and sister's care for the rest of their lives.

Lurana was given:

> *the use and improvement of the east half of the lower story of my Dwelling House, the East Porch, and South West Chamber, my Waggon-House, South Garden, and one third of the door-yard, three cords of wood yearly delivered in the door-yard and prepared for the fire and eighty dollars in cash yearly and I order my sons William A. Wilbour and Oliver H. Wilbour to keep her cows and horse (or any succeeding ones) equally between them.[58]*

Each of these items were given only as long as Lurana remained his widow and:

> *on condition of her allowing our Daughter Deborah a Home with her during her Widowhood and Deborah's celibacy ---- [59]*

Clarke's eldest and two youngest sons received land and money. His married daughters received money. His second son William A. and his third son Oliver H. were to split the Wilbor House and the farm. Clarke gave William the windmill and Judge William Wilbor's tall case clock. These gifts, too, were conditional; Oliver and William were to follow his instructions and care for their mother and sister. Thus Clarke maintained his control and care of his family even in death.

There is no probate inventory recording Clarke Wilbor's belongings, but when his wife Lurana passed away five years later in 1860, her very detailed inventory paints a vivid picture of their home. Clarke and Lurana were the first Wilbor House Wilbors to live in a way that was significantly different from their eighteenth- or even seventeenth-century ancestors. Change came very slowly to the Wilbor family home and presumably to other households in rural, isolated Little Compton. It was not until the mid-nineteenth century that expensive comforts like carpeting, easy chairs and carriages; or modern inventions like stoves, lamps and sinks made their way into the Wilbor household.

Lurana's inventory describes a comfortable "parlor" with a stove, carpets, mats, rocking chairs, a cloth-covered table, books and a clock. Another sitting room was carpeted and, among other things, included three "stuffed chairs," an "oil cloth" and two cloth-covered tables. The "East Bedroom" and "North Bedroom" were carpeted as well, and were furnished with a mix of old and new including a modern "washstand" and "bureau" alongside older-style chests, "high case drawers" and straw beds. Most exciting of all was the addition of a Victorian-era kitchen, perhaps after Clarke's death, that included a stove, a sink and a "refrigerator" (ice box). These modern innovations would have revolutionized the way the women of the house-hold performed their daily tasks. Far safer than cooking on a hearth, far more efficient than drawing water from a well, and at last enabling the family to eat fresh rather than preserved and salted foods, the new kitchen propelled the family into a new industrialized world. A long list of cleaning and laundry related items also indicates that this modern world was perhaps cleaner and more neatly pressed than the one that had come before.[60]

Sometime between 1850 and 1860 the Wilbors added not one, but two modern kitchens to their home, most likely around 1857 when William A. Wilbor married Susan B. Simmons. One kitchen replaced the seventeenth-century porch on the east side of the house. The other was added to the northwest corner of the house. When the new kitchens were added the eighteenth-century long kitchen was divided into small bedrooms that Carlton Brownell later described as "gloomy."[61]

The new northwest kitchen and a variety of other furnished rooms do not appear in Lurana's inventory as they were occupied by William, Susan and the unmarried Deborah. The 1860 Federal Census indicates that Lurana was living in a household with thirty-year-old Oliver, thirty-one-year-old Deborah, and Frederic Brownell, a fifteen-year-old hired boy who helped out on the farm. According to the census, William and Susan were their own separate household within the house.[62] Oliver H. Wilbor married Abby H. Manchester, nine years his junior, in December 1860, the same month of his mother's death. The couple established their household in the eastern rooms that were once Oliver's mother's. Though it is tempting to think that both new kitchens were built in honor of the Wilbor brides, Lurana's inventory makes it clear that the modern kitchen and its furnishings were hers before they were Oliver and Abby's.

Lurana's probate inventory also shows that the family was deeply involved in dairying and that the dairying business assets (as well as thirty-three hens and one cow) were hers and not her sons. The farm included a "milk room" that technically belonged to William and Oliver, but Lurana owned the equipment in it, including a churn, forty-one large tin pans, eight small tin pans, a milk and cream pail, a table and bench, trays and knife, brass skimmers, stone pots and other sundries. Certainly it was common for nineteenth-century families to own a cow for their own use, but Lurana's ownership of a total of forty-nine tin pans indicates that she was producing more product, most likely butter, than her family could use. It also suggests that she was processing the milk produced by her sons' cows as well as her own.

Lurana lived comfortably at the end of her life and had money to spare. As a result of her husband's assets as well as her own hard work, Lurana had over $400 deposited in a Tiverton bank. The male members of her family turned to her for loans, and at the time of her death she held notes from three of her sons including Oliver and William, as well as her twenty-nine-year-old cousin by marriage Isaac C. Wilbor. Isaac went on to become a very wealthy man. He was deeply involved in the development of the Rhode Island Red Hen, and around the turn of the twentieth century, his home, Prospect Hill Farm, became known as the largest poultry farm in the world. Perhaps this was in some small way due to the $25 he borrowed from his Cousin Lurana in 1860.[63]

THE SIXTH GENERATION —

William Andrew Wilbor (1827–1886) &
  Susan B. Simmons (1832–1883)
Deborah Wilbor (1829–1903)
Oliver Hazard Wilbor (1830–1906) &
  Abby H. Manchester (1839–1928)

When Lurana passed away she left a home that was, for the first time in its history, childless. Her daughter Deborah never married and neither of her sons William nor Oliver had children. Forty years later her daughter-

The Wilbor House. 1876. LCHS Collection

in-law, midwife Aunt Kate Wilbor would remark that many of Little Compton's Yankee residents were barren after far too many years of intermarriage. Only the Portuguese, she said, were having healthy babies.[64] Toward the end of the nineteenth century many of Little Compton's Yankee families were growing smaller due to lower birthrates and/or migration to areas with greater economic opportunities. Just as there were fewer and fewer Yankee sons to run Little Compton's farms there were more and more immigrant boys, especially Azoreans, eager for the opportunity to do so. Farms that had been owned by English colonists and their descendants for two hundred years were now beginning to pass into Portuguese hands.

An 1876 photograph of the Wilbor House (below) shows the sixth and final generation of Wilbor House Wilbors standing proudly in front of their family home wearing their best clothes and displaying their valuable

horses and carriage. There are far more people in the photograph than lived in the house at the time.[65] For an occasion as important as the creation of this photograph William, Susan, Oliver, Abby and Deborah were joined by relatives who lived nearby. Boarders and hired hands may also be pictured.

The photograph shows two young men in light brown farmers' smocks rather than the black suits worn by the other men. Both of these men seem to have dark complexions. In 1870 there were two black men living in Little Compton, neither one very close to the Wilbor House, but they had been joined by approximately twenty Western Islanders (Azores, Madeira, or Cape Verde) who were all recorded by the census taker as "mullatto."[66] It is possible that the men in the Wilbor House photo are dark-complexioned Portuguese, perhaps Cape Verdean. Like other laborers and servants, Little Compton's first Portuguese residents are not well documented in the local histories. Even those Azorean families that settled permanently in Little Compton escaped the notice of genealogist Benjamin Franklin Wilbour. His town-wide genealogy written between 1930 and 1960 contains only four Portuguese families, and in each of those four cases the head of the family married a woman of English descent. If these farm workers did not purchase land, marry, have children or break the law in Little Compton, they are essentially absent from the local historic record. Censuses provide the best opportunities to document their time in Little Compton.

William A. Wilbor continued to operate the mill his father had left him until his death in 1886.[67] Oliver farmed. Wives Susan and Abby were housekeepers, and Deborah alternated from housekeeper to seamstress at different times in her life.[68] Deborah was considered part of Abby and Oliver's household until Susan's death in 1883 when Deborah took over the housekeeping responsibilities for her widowed brother William. After William's death Deborah rejoined Oliver's household.[69]

The three Wilbor siblings and their spouses often had company in the Wilbor House. In addition to housing the hired boys working for Oliver, on at least one occasion the family rented a room to a boarder. Little Compton native, Mary F. Sisson, a twenty-nine-year-old school teacher was living in the Wilbor House in 1875.[70] Like most female teachers of the time, Mary was required to stay single in order to keep her job. The town of Little Compton paid the Wilbors for Mary's room and board, enabling her to walk to the one-room-school nearby. While she lived with the Wilbors Mary sewed a signature quilt most likely to raise money for the school. All the Wilbor family members signed the quilt which was recently loaned to the Historical Society.

Susan B. Simmons Wilbor was the first of the last Wilbor House Wilbors to pass away. She died at the age of fifty-one and had written her will ten months earlier indicating an illness and an expectation of early death. Though she left no probate inventory, her will contained very specific bequests to her Simmons family members that help detail the Wilbor House furnishings in 1883. These items include a silver candlestick, photographs, "two yellow bottomed chairs," a cake box, and two quilts or "pieced spreads" one in "brickwork and the other in stars and stripes." Niece Susie Simmons was given a dozen silver spoons marked "SBS" and Linnie Simmons received three silver spoons marked "LS." This is the first time that items like patchwork quilts and photographs appear in the home's furnishings. Susan and school teacher Mary Sisson may have passed many evenings together working on their patchwork quilts. As an in-law with no children of her own, Susan was free, both legally and socially, to give her personal belongings and over $550 in cash to her blood-relations rather than to her Wilbor in-laws, and that is just what she chose to do. The only Wilbor mentioned in her will was her husband William, whom she named executor and left the "rest and residue."[71]

William passed away three years later at the age of fifty-nine. His will, too, was written at a young age, approximately one year before his death, indicating a final year filled with serious illness. William's 1886 probate inventory describes a comfortable home with an abundance of space for his family of two. William and Susan's western portion of the Wilbor House included a carpeted and rather cluttered sitting room with a tall clock inherited from his great-uncle Judge William Wilbor, a sewing machine, eight chairs, four rocking chairs, a lounge, two tables, a looking glass, books and pictures hanging on the wall. They also had a parlor with six additional wooden chairs, a rocker, a "stuffed" chair and a table. There were three bedrooms including a "lower bedroom" with a bed, bureau and washstand; a more elaborate "upper bedroom" that was carpeted and contained slightly more expensive furniture; and an "attic bedroom" filled with chests and used at this point in their lives primarily for storage. The attic bedroom exists today in an unrestored state and is a very pleasant, though unheated, space. It could have provided a private place for hired help or boarders to stay. William's modern kitchen was equipped with a stove and an extension table. There was also a "Porch Chamber" likely the small attic room over the new kitchen extension. At the time of his death William had recently purchased ten yards of new carpet. He owned two stoves and had a bank account with over $700.

Unlike the five generations of Wilbor fathers before him, William had no direct descendants to inherit the Wilbor House and farm. He also knew that his brother, housemate and business partner Oliver would soon be in a similar situation. Though he had numerous relatives who lived in Little Compton and might have carried on the tradition of Wilbors in the Wilbor House, William focused instead on his two surviving brothers as his heirs. A generation earlier Clarke and Lurana Wilbor produced six sons. Together, those six men produced only a single male heir, Herbert Clarke Wilbor, a resident of New Bedford who did not want a farm in Little Compton. William wrote in his will:

- *To Brother Oliver the use and improvement of all my real estate during his life & at his death I give and bequeath my real estate to my two brothers Alexander C. Wilbour and Alfred G. Wilbour equally.*

- *Provided they or their legal representatives pay to my sister Deborah Wilbor yearly and every year one third of the rents and profits of said real estate during her natural life and not otherwise.*

- *Brother Oliver all my stock farming tools, carriages and farm products on hand at the time of my decease to him and his heirs.*

- *My personal property except what is otherwise disposed of I give to my brothers Alexander C. Wilbour and Alfred G. Wilbour, my sister Deborah Wilbour, and my two nieces Caroline C. Brown and Mattie H. Wilbour to be equally divided between them.*[72]

Not much is known about Deborah after William's death. William ensured that she would continue to be provided for, and she lived with

Oliver and Abby until her death in 1903 at the age of seventy-four. Deborah, however, left no will or probate inventory to reveal her last wishes or list her personal belongings.

Oliver did not provide much more information when he passed away in 1906 at seventy-six years of age. He wrote his will in 1900 when his sister Deborah was still alive and provided her with the same income we see in William's earlier will. He also chose the same heirs as William to inherit his portion of the family farm. Oliver appointed his wife Abby as his executrix and left her all of his personal property, but he failed to provide Abby with any sort of lifelong residency at the Wilbor House.[73] It is odd that someone would provide so carefully for a sister but leave his wife's future uncertain. Abby lived another twenty-two years beyond her husband's death and spent much of it at the Wilbor House.

Oliver Wilbor. LCHS Collection.

The new owners of the Wilbor House, Oliver's brother Alfred, and Martha Blaine the only surviving child of his brother George, were uninterested in living in Little Compton and were content to let Abby stay as long as she liked.

Abby did not live alone, at least for long. In 1910 she was sharing a portion of the house with the growing Fagundes family who were Azorean immigrants.[74]

Manuel, 35, arrived 1903
Jessie, 25, arrived 1904
Emmaline, 4
Manuel, 3
Mary, 4 months
Father-in-law Frank Mayo, 55, arrived 1907
Mother-in-law, Claudine, 45, arrived 1907

Fagundes descendants have told the Little Compton Historical Society that Manuel and Jessie worked at the Wilbor House and lived in the attic over the northwest kitchen. There are traces of wall paper on the south wall of that attic room as well as an opening for a stove pipe that indicate it was used as livable space sometime in the past. Manuel worked on the farm and Jessie worked in the house.[75] By 1910, Oliver had passed away and the Fagundes family had grown from two to seven, leading to their use of half of the house. By 1920 the Fagundes had moved on, and eighty-year-old Abby was living in the house by herself. Though the details are not clear, it is believed that Abby moved to New Bedford to be closer to family until her death in 1928. She was the last Wilbor to live in the Wilbor House.

The Fagundes Family. Courtesy of Catherine Fagundes Silvia.

THE TENANCY YEARS

The Wilbor heirs sold the family home and its sixty acre farm to Manuel DeAlmo for $1,000 "and other valuable considerations" in 1919.[76] Like many Little Compton deeds this one preserved the new owner's right to cross his neighbors' land in order to collect seaweed for fertilizer and wintertime insulation. DeAlmo was an Azorean immigrant who was interested in the property not because of the house but because of its large barn. DeAlmo established a dairy farm at the Wilbor farm and rented the Wilbor House to tenants for the next thirty-five years.

The house changed very little during the tenancy period. Carlton Brownell noted that many of the home's original features including floorboards, feather-edged siding and brick fireplaces were still there covered by layers of plaster, paint and wall paper.[77] The home including three apartments that made use of the dividing walls constructed by the Wilbors during their many years of shared living. Though it is possible that the configuration of the apartments changed during the tenancy years, it is most likely that there was a single, large upstairs apartment occupying the whole floor and two smaller downstairs apartments, one on the west side in the 1740 addition and one on the east side in the original 1690 structure. What is important to remember is that the Wilbor House started functioning as an apartment-style dwelling in the early 1700s when the first Wilbor daughter-in-law moved in. The tenancy years carried on that tradition.

Manuel DeAlmo purchased the Wilbor House in 1919. LCHS Collection.

Because Little Compton census records of the period do not use house numbers it is challenging to determine who lived in the Wilbor House from 1920 to 1935. Local residents remember Wilbor House tenants from the 1940s and 50s and have shared their stories with us. The 1930 Federal census shows that the Pontes and the Littlefield families were renting in the neighborhood, but whether or not they rented Wilbor House apartments is unclear. The 1940 Census places George and Mary Flores at the Wilbor House and shows that they were in the same apartment in 1935. The 1940 Census also indicates that their fellow tenants may have been seventy-four-year-old Frederick Johnson, a glass bottle salesman, and his fifty-four-year-old secretary Louise Lawton. An unmarried couple sharing an apartment most likely raised a few eyebrows in 1940 Little Compton, but it makes sense that Manuel DeAlmo, a successful dairy farmer, would have been the business associate and landlord of a glass bottle salesman.

Johnson reported that he worked only twenty-five hours per week and listed an annual income of over $5,000, an enormous sum compared to his West Main Road neighbors. Everyone else in the immediate neighborhood listed an income of $950 or less per year. Mary Flores was working seventy-two hours each week as a cook for the Brayton family across the street. Her annual income was $390. Manuel DeAlmo charged the Flores $8 per month for rent. He charged Frederick Johnson $30.

Angelina Ferreira, a divorced mother of two, rented the second floor apartment for herself and her children Frannie and Manuel from the early 1940s until the early 1950s. Angelina worked hard as a maid for local

Frannie Ferreira's wedding reception, 1948.
Courtesy of Carolyn Montgomery

families, and the Wilbor House offered an affordable place for her family to live. It was close enough to her work that she could manage without a car. Manny served in the military and took advantage of the G.I. Bill to graduate from Cornell University. Frannie was married while living at the Wilbor House, and her wedding photo shows the electric meters for the building's three apartments in the background.

Frannie remembers the Nunes family living in the west (or front) downstairs apartment and George and Mary Flores still living in the downstairs apartment to the rear (east).

For many years, the Wilbor House apartments used hand pumps for water in the kitchens and outhouses for bathrooms, but by the 1950s there was modern running water and at least one toilet in the house. Outhouses were not uncommon on Little Compton farms in the 1940s. The O'Neil family and the Heywood-Wood family rented two Wilbor House apartments in the 1950s and have happy memories of their times there.[78]

BECOMING A MUSEUM

In the 1950s the Little Compton Historical Society was an organization in search of a headquarters. A building search committee gave serious consideration to the Friends Meeting House, the Peckham House on Peckham Lot at the Commons, now demolished, as well as the Wilbor House. Committee member Miles Richmond called the building "The Wood House" in his report to the society, referring to the Heywood-Wood family and described the house as follows:

*a building of historical and architectural interest which would make
a fitting background for the articles now owned by the society and
those which might be loaned to it for exhibition purposes. It now has
two apartments on the first floor and one on the second floor…Looking
forward to the future both the house and the contents should be of
sufficient interest to the public to justify an admission fee and it should
be possible for a caretaker to live on the premises.[79]*

In a separate report Carlton Brownell called the house "The Oliver
Wilbor House" and reported:

*The upstairs apartment is in very good repair and hired by Mr. Wood
and his wife who have painted and papered it. There is also another
apartment at the east which is not in so good repair and another at the
west. It would be possible for the Historical Society to let the upstairs
apartment and the one at the east and to use the west apartment for
themselves. This last has four rooms. Mr. DiAlmo (sic) owns the place
and is offering the house and the yard for sale for fifteen thousand. There
is a mortgage of eight thousand five hundred dollars on the whole place.*

*A far more suitable building than the Peckham House. In form and
detail it resembles the Bessie Gray House. The east end is probably late
17th century, the west not more than a hundred years later. Early
fireplace framings, hewn timbers, original floors, doors and woodwork
exist to a great extent.[80]*

Brownell concluded his report discouragingly, "It is unlikely the
Historical Society could purchase it without unforeseen help."

With no donor in sight, the organization let go of its hope of using the
Wilbor House as a headquarters and focused instead on finding a private
person "someone desiring to own an ancient dwelling. Such houses have
been in some demand, perhaps we can help a suitable owner in putting
the house back into shape as a home of great historic interest."[81]

Luck, however, intervened and Mrs. Dorothy Brayton, the across the
street neighbor now living in Onegan, offered funds to purchase the house.
Carlton recalls that she was distressed by the appearance of the house and

its yard. The Society acquired the property for $8,000 in 1955 and spent the next two years and $28,000 restoring it.[82]

Carlton Brownell played a critical role in the restoration of the Wilbor House. His detailed description of the work done to the house appears on page 53.

On August 25, 1957 the Historical Society opened the Wilbor House Museum to the public and welcomed 150 people on opening day. During its first year 400 people visited the Wilbor House and paid twenty-five cents for the tour.

Only a portion of the downstairs was open to the public in 1957. Carlton Brownell recalled that the house committee decided not to open the 1850 Victorian Kitchen to the public because it was "too new" and would not be of interest. The upstairs was reserved for a caretaker. Miss Edna Gray became the first resident caretaker and hostess in 1955. Historical Society meeting notes report that she "has a most attractive and homelike apartment."[83] Due in large part to Carlton's continued devotion to the museum, the Victorian Kitchen and three upstairs rooms were eventually furnished with period pieces and opened to the public. Today the Wilbor House Museum welcomes over 3,000 visitors each year to tour nine authentically-furnished rooms and to hear the story of an ordinary Little Compton family.

Over the course of 250 years the home sheltered multiple generations not as a single household but as separate family units occupying discreet apartments within the building. The need for these apartments began in the first half of the eighteenth century requiring multiple additions and the construction of dividing walls within the older rooms of the house. The house also served, from the very beginning, not just as a farmhouse but as a place of secondary businesses, including a weaving shop, a doctor's office, a shoemaker's shop, a dairy, a seamstress shop and a boarding house.

In four different centuries the Wilbor House was a home, a place of business and a safety net for a hard-working, extended, middle-class family. The personal stories of its patriarchs, its housewives, its children, servants and tenants are representative of other men, women and children in the Little Compton community and so help visitors understand the history of not just a house but a town.

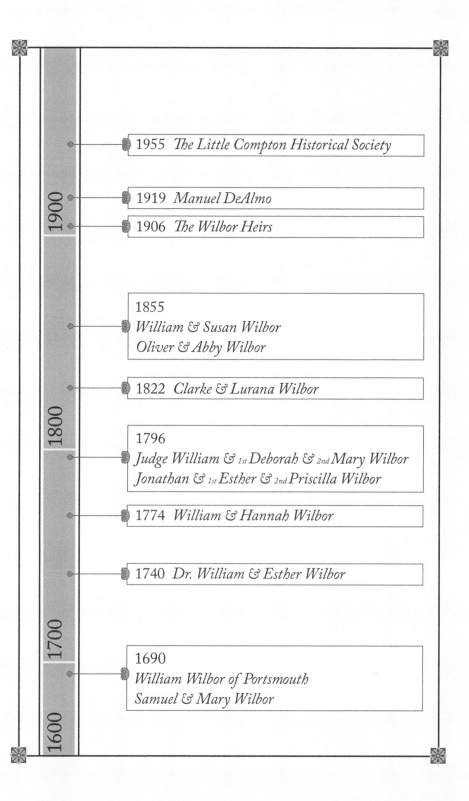

1955 *The Little Compton Historical Society*

1919 *Manuel DeAlmo*

1906 *The Wilbor Heirs*

1855
William & Susan Wilbor
Oliver & Abby Wilbor

1822 *Clarke & Lurana Wilbor*

1796
Judge William & 1st Deborah & 2nd Mary Wilbor
Jonathan & 1st Esther & 2nd Priscilla Wilbor

1774 *William & Hannah Wilbor*

1740 *Dr. William & Esther Wilbor*

1690
William Wilbor of Portsmouth
Samuel & Mary Wilbor

1900

1800

1700

1600

Wilbor House Restoration and Fundraising Committee Members, 1957, from left to right, Carlton Brownell, Miles Richmond, David Brayton, Doctor Whitmarsh and B.F. Wilbour. LCHS Collection.

The Restoration of the Wilbor House

By Carlton C. Brownell

The restoration of the Wilbor House began in 1955 when Mrs. David A. Brayton presented it to the Little Compton Historical Society. The President of the Society, Doctor Robert H. Whitmarsh, appointed Carlton C. Brownell, Miles S. Richmond, and David A. Brayton as a Committee of Restoration. Isaac C. Bliss was selected as general contractor. Plans for restoration and supervision of work were by Carlton Brownell. Skilled reconstructions in brick, stone, wood and iron were done by local craftsmen.

Nearly all early details of the house were present, although masked by later work. Beamed ceilings, feather-edge boards and original plaster had been covered by new plaster after studs were inserted. This had been done for insulation but was removed as not needed for museum purposes. Doors, floorboards, moldings, etc., which were missing or badly mutilated were replaced from several Little Compton houses which had been recently demolished. Some millwork was copied from remnants still in place.

Throughout its history the house remained simple and plain. Although ultimately of large size, there was never anything of the mansion about it. All details are simple to the point of severity. Its interest and importance lies in its being a typical home of New England for many generations.

LOWER GREAT ROOM *c.1690*

The large stone fireplace of the lower great room is a restoration based on evidence discovered when a brick fireplace identical with the existing one on the west was removed. The original stone fireplace had almost straight sides but the reconstruction had to be angled in order not to

LCHS Collection.

destroy the original eighteenth-century fireplace in the north room, which must have been built after the original stone chimney, was removed. The present chimney of brick and stone is eighteenth century.

Late plaster and laths were removed from the ceilings of both older rooms and the north room (Upper & Lower Great Room & the Long Kitchen). Beneath the plaster was found whitewash on the boards and joists, but under the whitewash was the sooty black discoloration of a hundred years of fireplace smoke. This is the dark color, which shows on the ceiling of the lower rooms. Upstairs the wood is lighter as second floor fireplaces were used much less often as is shown by the better condition of brickwork in almost all upper rooms of old houses.

During the restoration late partitions were removed to return the rooms to their original size. Both of the oldest rooms had been divided into three parts. Few of the partitions were of much age, but in the lower great room a north-south wall of wide vertical boards seemed to be eighteenth century. As this room had served as kitchen, dining room, living room and sometimes bedroom to the first generations of Wilbors, it was probably divided as soon as the north room (Long Kitchen) was built.

UPPER GREAT ROOM *c.1690*

The upper great room retains much original work as well as some of the early-eighteenth century. The small joists running into a large summer beam are seventeenth century as are the posts and braces. Two braces had to be replaced because they were cut through for a closet door on the north and for a sash window on the south. Feather-edge boarding was in place. The fireplace and over-panel may be later than the room but were not changed as they are of great age. Most of the plaster was replaced but one section of the old remains. Plaster was thickly covered with whitewash. Around the bottom of the room was a six-inch border of blue-black color. No baseboards of any age were found.

The casement windows (in the Upper and Lower Great Rooms) are reconstructions based on openings found in the wall and similar windows in houses of the same age. An exact opening was found patched on the upper south side and signs of one on the east. No evidence was found in the lower room as large sash windows had destroyed the early opening. The braces of the upper room limited windows to the center of the walls, but on the lower floor the absence of braces made more space. In 1991 the leaded casement windows were re-made to conform to further study.

Since the house when built only had two rooms, besides an attic and east ell now gone, the large downstairs room served all living purposes, including bedroom for the parents.

HALLWAY *c.1740*

The stairs took all the space in the first hall and a door entered directly out of the great room at the southwest corner, where signs can still be seen. The present entrance reproduces one built after the enlargement of the entry around 1740. An entrance of about 1850 had sidelights and a large door. This was removed in the restoration of 1956 when the plaster was removed from the feather-edge boards of the north wall. As now seen, the hall is as it was in the early-eighteenth century.

SOUTHWEST SITTING ROOM *c.1740*

The ceilings in the west rooms, up and down, are constructed in the same manner as the older rooms, but investigation showed the wood to be clean and light colored, having always been covered by the present plaster ceilings.

LONG KITCHEN, KITCHEN BEDROOM & PANTRY *c.1740*

The large north room (Long Kitchen) is all of early construction but the details suggest that it was not all added at once. The section directly north of the great room may have been the first addition and possibly had a shed or "salt box" roof. The fireplace with bake oven in the north rooms shows that that room then became the kitchen (after the Lower Great Room). Later, this room was divided and the ells were built as kitchens.

Feather-edge board partitions forming a very small room (Kitchen Bedroom) and a pantry at the west end of the long north kitchen have been replaced as marks of the vertical boards and positions of doors were clearly seen. Signs of shelf positions also show around the northwest corner post. During the last half of the nineteenth century the long room was divided into dark, cramped, bedrooms opening one into the other. The fireplace was bricked in and shallow clothes closets backed up to the brick work. The rooms were exceedingly gloomy and drab, each having one north window.

Some window positions in the lower north room (Long Kitchen) show signs of relocation to make way for the north ell (Victorian Kitchen).

SOUTHWEST CHAMBER *c.1740*

Brick work in the chimneys and fireplaces on the west and north is eighteenth century. The upper west room is unchanged, even the green paint replicates the first paint found under many later coats.

NORTHWEST CHAMBER *c.1740*

In the small, upper, northwest room, the plaster is recent. A fire must have started in this room and quickly put out as charred portions of the feather-edge partition were lathed and plastered. When the plaster was removed the burn marks were as fresh as when the fire was put out. In this room a door into the nineteenth-century attic (over the Victorian Kitchen) replaces a window.

The north side of the Wilbor House. LCHS Collection

BACK STAIRS

The back stairs show clear evidence of having been turned in the opposite direction to what they now face, and in the cellar stone steps end against the floor.

OPEN CHAMBER

The middle upper room was unfinished until the nineteenth century, it having been what is called locally "the open chamber." These unplastered upper rooms were used for storage or bedrooms for hired men or boys of the family.

ATTIC

In the attic it is possible to trace changes and additions by noting different directions of floorboards. Rafters, too, show evidence of having been lengthened by pegging on new sections to extend the roof over later rooms. The first roof had but three pairs of rafters with horizontal purlins holding boards running from peak to eves in a manner derived from thatching methods. These original rafters are still here, turned over and lengthened. Other hewn oak rafters are also present as well as twentieth-century two-by-sixes added by the owner preceding the Historical Society.

WINDOWS

The sash windows of the eighteenth-century sections were copied from originals, some in place, others stored in the attic. The large size of the wooden bars, or muntins, is typical of this period. Evidence was found that all north windows, up and down, were originally very small. They were like the smallest one in the upper north middle room (Open Chamber). This is an original frame and sash. As the north side of the house is not of a period to have had casement windows, these small sash windows were the first ones on the back of the house. The usual custom was the placing of smaller windows at the rear with larger ones at the front. Almost without exception glass size would be the same but with varying numbers of lights. It will be noticed that lower windows in the eighteenth-century portion of the house are one row of lights taller than on the upper floor. Although all frames of sash windows show the same heavy construction, the upper ones on the front show more weathering under the paint than on the lower floor, which would seem to indicate that the lower frames were replaced. If so, it must have been early in the history of this part of the house.

WALLS

The earliest wallpaper found in the house dates after 1830. Every room showed many coats of whitewash on plaster and sometimes on wood. Most rooms had a painted base border.

Feather-edge boarding in the front hall, the Lower Great Room, the upper northwest bedroom and the Upper Great Room is all original to the house. Feather-edge boarding in the large north room (Long Kitchen) at the east end and over the fireplace was so damaged that it had to be replaced.

The Waite-Potter house in Westport, Massachusetts, which was demolished in the 1954 hurricane, was purchased and materials used in the north room. Part of the floor of the oldest lower room is also from the Waite-Potter house as are some batten doors throughout the house. The two-room stone-ender known as the Waite-Potter house is thought to have been the only house in the area to escape destruction in the Indian wars of 1675. If so, it was a few years older than the Wilbor House.

Waite Potter House, Westport, c.1950. LCHS Collection.

Clapboards on the front of the house were copied from originals on the Amasa Gray house, also seventeenth century. Clapboards on the front and shingles on the side are a local building custom from an early date.

VICTORIAN KITCHENS *c.1850*

Two ells were added to serve as kitchens. The eastern ell (now part of the Reception Room) was built c.1850. It replaced a smaller ell on the same site. The roofline of the older building once could be seen in the attic of the newer addition. This small, steep-roofed "porch" may have been the first part built. The proportions were like those of the first houses at Plymouth. It was a summer kitchen for many years. Abby Manchester Wilbor, widow of Oliver H. Wilbor, states that, "There was a small porch with one window of diamond panes of glass moved off when the new porch was added." The similar north ell, shown as our Victorian Kitchen, also dates from about 1850 and has not been altered.

RECEPTION ROOM *c.1967*

In 1967 an addition was made to the east end of Wilbor House, incorporating the 1850 ell. The addition was provided for in the will of

Benjamin Franklin Wilbour to serve as a display area. The addition is named for Mr. Wilbour's father and mother, The Benjamin Franklin and Clara Brown Wilbour Memorial. In design it conforms to Little Compton buildings of the mid-eighteenth century. The stair balusters are copies of early-eighteenth-century ones once in the B.F. Wilbour house. Balusters of the same design were also used in the Congregational Church of 1724.

FURNISHINGS

Furnishings in the Wilbor House consist of gifts and loans from various sources. Although, little that was used in the house has been located, the Society has many items used in Little Compton during the periods that the house represents. Since a large number of the furnishings have come from Wilbor descendants, it is possible that some may have been in the house before.

OUTBUILDINGS

Seventeenth-century farm buildings were small and roughly built. Farming was subsistence with little for sale so farm animals were few in number and equipment and vehicles were very limited. As living standards rose and more was produced for sale, the old buildings were swept away and replaced and are quite rare today. With agriculture in steady decline in New England, even much later farm buildings are rapidly vanishing.

Carlton Brownell and workers restoring the Wilbor House Barn. LCHS Collection.

The outhouse (privy) is partly seventeenth century. The carriage house, corncrib, barn and cookhouse are nineteenth-century buildings. The carriage house is original to the property and contains restored vehicles, including a one-horse shay and a sleigh. The corn crib and cookhouse were moved to the property.

Corn was an essential food for people and livestock and distinctive buildings, called corncribs, evolved for storing it. For ventilation, floors or walls were slatted and the corncrib was raised on stone posts to discourage rats from reaching the corn.

Manuel DeAlmo moved the nineteenth-century barn to the east, raised it over a cellar, and extended it to the east and operated a large dairy farm there from about 1928 to 1950. In later years the barn was used by the growers of Brownell Roses until it was eventually purchased by the Historical Society.

The Society now uses the barn as a museum for old vehicles and tools. Besides farm articles, there are displays of equipment related to laundry, dairy, shoe repairing, fishing, and spinning and weaving. There is also a room commemorating the heritage of the Portuguese who settled in Little Compton in the middle and late-nineteenth century.

The Rhode Island Red chicken was developed and named in Little Compton. After 1850 poultry raising became a farm industry by itself. Before that time farmers kept a few chickens just for their own use. It was believed locally that chickens benefited from cooked food, so for about forty years every farm had a "cook house" where chicken food was prepared for the Rhode Island Reds. On display is an 1870 cookhouse with equipment.

Near the barn is an 1850 catboat with a curious "cabin." Sydney Burleigh (1853-1931), a local artist, rescued the abandoned boat, moved it to his yard and built a thatched superstructure for a studio. He named it "Peggotty." Many years later it was moved to the Society's grounds.

A replica of the town's first school house is on the grounds. Early schools were in private homes until the first schoolhouse was built on the Commons in 1725, and later moved to several sites on West Road according to where the largest number of children lived. Pupils were of all grades but learning did not go much beyond reading and writing. One-room schools continued in use until 1929. The first schoolhouse was named Peaked Top and went out of use around 1860. However several former pupils wrote very complete descriptions of the building and school life and many paintings exist of it, so in 1975 a replica was built for the town's 300th anniversary. It contains books, slates, and other items used in the early schools.

The herb garden was designed, and is maintained, by the Little Compton Garden Club. For over fifty years members of the Little Compton Garden Club have continuously tended the symmetrically planted twenty-foot by twenty-foot plot which sustains approximately forty different herbs and plants grown in Colonial gardens. While Colonial herb gardens were formal in design, the herbs were often intermingled with flowers and vegetables, unlike the European ones. The symmetrical layout, stone-wall enclosure, and clamshell walkways were usually associated with a more sophisticated city home rather than a farm dwelling such as the Wilbor House. However, the same herbs and plants were grown in rural land-scapes as well, and used in everyday life for home remedies, to soothe and heal the sick and for cooking.

In 2002 the Historical Society moved a very early eighteenth-century barn from Topsfield, Massachusetts to the property and protected it with new exterior construction. The barn contains the society's archives and changing exhibit space.

The Wilbor House Museum, c. 1960. LCHS Collection.

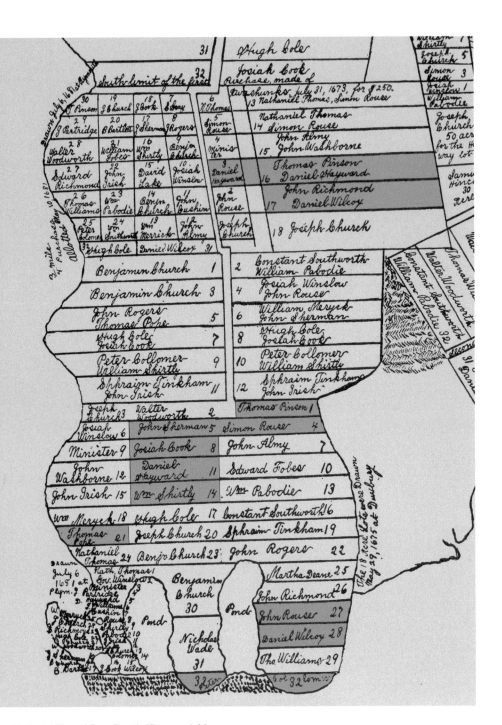

Nathaniel Warren's Lots. Detail of Proprietor's Map.

One Proprietor Six Historic Houses

SEACONNET HOUSE • LUNT HOUSE •
MARSH HOUSE • HUNTOON HOUSE •
STROBELL-GOODRICH COTTAGE •
SEABURY HOUSE

By Marjory O'Toole

Nathaniel Warren

Nathaniel Warren of Plymouth was not one of Sakonnet's First Proprietors, but he was one of the very first young English men to settle here. Between 1690 and 1700 he purchased hundreds of acres in lots scattered all over Little Compton from Sakonnet Point to Quicksand Pond. While researching the histories of the houses to be included in the Little Compton Historical Society's 2015 historic house tour we discovered that six of those houses occupy land that was once owned by Nathaniel Warren, an amazing coincidence that highlights the central role a handful of men played in establishing the town.

Each historic home helps illustrate important aspects of Little Compton's history from the prominence of weaving in the eighteenth century, to the earliest moments of the summer community in the nineteenth century, to the creative repurposing of buildings into family homes in the twentieth. We are pleased to present their remarkably interwoven histories here.

Like all Little Compton properties the story of Nathaniel Warren's land begins long before the arrival of English Proprietors with the Sakonnet Indians. Little Compton's Proprietors acquired this particular land as part of the second purchase made in 1675 that included the entire southwest portion of the town. Each of the twenty-nine First Proprietors drew lots for a fifty-acre parcel, an eighteen-acre lot and a tiny sliver of Sakonnet Harbor. The eighteen-acre lots stretched from the Sakonnet River across what is now Sakonnet Golf Club to include all of Warren's Point. The Proprietors called this area the "Common Field." Nathaniel Warren bought his lots from several First Proprietors including Joseph Church and William Fobes. Warren also acquired three-eighths of a share in the proprietorship which made him a proprietor in his own right and gave him a right to participate in the future purchase of Indian lands east of the "Cole Brook line."[1]

By Little Compton standards, where many families live for six, seven, even eight generations, Nathaniel Warren and his wife Phebe Murdock did not stay for very long. The couple had no children and moved from Little Compton to Newport around 1700 and eventually back to Plymouth.[2] The Warrens did, however, make a lasting mark on the community by lending their name to the "neck" of land on which they built their home, Warren's Point.

THE COES & THE SEABURY HOUSE

In 1693 the Warren's sold land just south of the Wilbor House Museum to John Coe.[3] This land would eventually become the site of the Seabury House described in the book on page 156.

THE BAILEY FAMILY FARMS

Patriarch John Bailey

Four years later, in March of 1697/98[4] Nathaniel Warren sold his homestead farm on Warren's Point along with its nearby land to John Bailey of Portsmouth.[5] In the seven short years the Warrens lived on the Point they made tremendous improvements to their property creating a farm that was described in the deed as containing "stables, outhouses, sheds, shops and all manner of buildings upon them with all the dwelling houses, barns with all the orchard gardens and fruit trees." It was this well-improved homestead farm that attracted the attention of the Bailey family and eventually became the site of five of the homes described in this book.

John Bailey, a successful farmer from Portsmouth, Rhode Island, was eager to secure farms for his sons even though they were still young boys.

The Bailey House on Warren's Point. Postcard by O.E. Dubois. LCHS Collection.

His 1697 purchase of nine eighteen-acre lots from Nathaniel Warren ensured that there would be good land available when his sons came of age. Until then it is likely that tenant farmers continued "the use and improvement" of the land and produced an additional stream of income for the Bailey family. Eventually John gave the lots on what is now called Bailey's Ledge to his son William and the lots at Warren's Point, or "The Neck" as it was sometimes called, to his son Thomas. John, however, like many colonial fathers did not formalize this gift until after his death when his will was proved in 1736.[6]

Thomas and Mary Bailey's farm at Warren's Point eventually became the site of three of the homes featured in this book – Lunt House, Seaconnet House and Marsh House – while two other historic homes, the Strobell-Goodrich Cottage and the Huntoon House, were built on land once owned by William and Dorothy Bailey. The shared house histories that follow will trace the story of the Bailey farms from the seventeenth century until the twenty-first, branching off as each new home appears on the historic landscape.

Please see page 68 to continue the story of the Baileys of Warrens Point and The Seaconnet House, the Marsh House and the Lunt House.

Please see page 116 to continue the story of the Baileys of Bailey Ledge and the Huntoon House, The Orchard and the Strobell-Goodrich Cottage.

Portrait of Mary Bailey Richmond. *Courtesy of James Lynch.*

The Baileys of Warren's Point

THREE SONS, THREE FARMS

By Marjory O'Toole

Lieutenant Thomas Bailey (1690–1741) &
Mary Wood (1691–1745)

Thomas and Mary Bailey once owned almost all of Warren's Point from the Atlantic Ocean to the intersection of what would someday be called West Main Road, Sakonnet Point Road and Warren's Point Road. A very early house known as the Thomas Bailey House, and often referred to as one of the oldest in Little Compton, still sits near the gate to Warren's Point. As old as this home may be, it is unlikely that it is the first house constructed by Nathaniel Warren which would have had a more seventeenth-century appearance. Thomas' heirs would soon add even more land to the family holdings by purchasing the adjacent farms to the north and lands to the west. Thomas was born in 1690 perhaps in Portsmouth, Rhode Island. At the age of twenty-two he married Mary Wood in Little Compton in 1712 and likely moved to Warren's Point at that time. Over the course of the next twenty years they welcomed ten children, nine boys in a row and finally one daughter whom they named after her mother.

Like a number of Bailey men, Thomas died young leaving his widow and adult sons to manage the farm and care for the family's six minor children. He must have known the end was near, writing his will in January 1741 and passing away the following April at the age of fifty-one. Benjamin Franklin Wilbour describes Thomas as "the richest man in town." His wealth was due in part to the richness of his land as well as the labor of three enslaved African or African American people who appear in his probate inventory: Vilo who (perhaps because of her age) was worth a

The Thomas Bailey House, Warren's Point. Etching by Richard Kinnicutt, 1937. Print by Josie Richmond Arkins, 2010.

modest 34 £, Phillis who was valued at 100 £, and Crawco a boy (perhaps Phillis' child) who was not given a value.[1] Because Thomas did not specifically mention Vilo, Phillis and Crawco in his will they would have been considered a part of his personal property and distributed one third to his widow Mary and two thirds to his children. The fate of Vilo, Phillis and Crawco is unclear, but the Baileys continued to own slaves through 1790.[2]

Thomas provided handsomely for his wife and his children, but saved the formal division of the family farm for a later date when his youngest son Samuel turned twenty-one. The children divided their father's Warren's Point farm and nearby lands around 1753.[3] The two oldest sons John and Thomas elected to stay and farm the family land. John received the land on the northern edge of Warren's Point on which Seaconnet House now stands and was the first to build a home there. Thomas, the second son, was given his father's homestead farm and lived on Warren's Point itself.

Just two years after officially receiving their share, four of the boys chose to make their fortune elsewhere and sold their lots to a blacksmith from Newport named Oliver White. White's land sat in between John's and Thomas' and would be referred to as the "White Farm" for many years to come, even once the Baileys bought it back. Had all the brothers stayed in "The Neck" their small farms may not have led to prosperous futures. Constant Bailey (spelled Bealey in the deed) sold Oliver White twelve acres and farmed instead in Tiverton, closer to his wife's family, the Almys. His brothers may have given up farming all together. Joseph Bailey of Newport a Cordwainer sold twelve and a half acres. Oliver Bailey of Tiverton a Clothier sold eleven and three-quarter acres. Barzilla Bailey a Mariner of Newport sold eighty-four acres. Their sister Mary also received a share through her husband. Stephen Pain a Mariner of Bristol and husband of Mary Pain sold ten acres to Oliver White on the same day as the Bailey brothers. It was very unusual for daughters to inherit land from their fathers at this time. Mary's husband Stephen would have become the legal owner of all her real estate the moment they were married. For these Bailey siblings leaving town and pursuing other professions had far more appeal than staying on the family land. Their professional choices are an interesting window into the options available to New England's eighteenth-century sons who for lack of land or lack of interest chose not to be farmers.[4]

Why Barzilla received so much more land than his siblings is unknown. There are numerous examples in Little Compton probate records of fathers dividing their property evenly among their children. Sons usually received real estate while daughters were given household goods. Surprisingly, due to the low value of land and the high cost of furniture and textiles the difference between the boys' and the girls' inheritances was not as great as if the same customs were followed today. It is possible that Thomas' other sons received money or personal property to make up for the difference in land. Little Compton's records also show examples of children being favored or even disinherited, so this particular disparity in inheritance remains a mystery.

In total Oliver White purchased just over 130 acres in the heart of Bailey territory, the equivalent of seven eighteen-acre lots, but the story of the White Farm is a short one lasting just thirty-seven years. John Bailey's son Isaac bought the entire farm back from Oliver White's heirs in 1792 and would later give it to his son Tillinghast. The White Farm would eventually become the location of the Marsh House. (Please see pg. 88 for the history of the Marsh House.)

John Bailey (1713–1777) &
Mary Wheaton (1721–1778)

Thomas and Mary's eldest son John also died at the relatively young age of sixty-three in 1777, but not before increasing the size of the farm his father left him by buying twenty-two acres of land and a house to the north from William and Perez Richmond in 1771 and 1775.[5] John considered himself not just a yeoman, a land-owning farmer, but a gentleman, a wealthy man who owned the land but did not work it himself.[6]

John Bailey married another Mary, Mary Wheaton of Swansea in 1740 and likely built his own home around that time on the east side of the intersection of Warren's Point Road, West Main Road and Sakonnet Point Road. John and Mary had only three children, an unusually small number for the time. Their only daughter Deborah was married and living in her own home at the time of their deaths. In his will John left his eldest son Isaac the homestead farm that would become Seaconnet House as well as the responsibility for the care of his mother and younger brother John. His father's will required Isaac to provide his mother "all things Needfull and Necessary." Mary died only a year after her husband. At the time of his parents' deaths Isaac was married to Sarah Manchester and was the father of two small children. Isaac and Sarah most likely lived with John and Mary in the family home, as did Isaac's younger brother John who at age nineteen had not yet left the nest. Like the Wilbor House, the Bailey House sheltered multiple generations at one time and grew and changed with the family's changing needs.

While writing his will, John the elder was most concerned about his son John who was unmarried, without an heir and fighting in the American Revolution. Among other things John inherited a farm of approximately forty acres and a house formerly occupied by Isaac Southworth just to the north of his father's homestead. Twenty-two acres of this property and the house were purchased from the Richmonds.[7] John also was given his father's slave Kuffe. It is likely that Kuffe was experienced with the workings of the Bailey farm. Perhaps Kuffe brought with him a measure of maturity and experience that the nineteen-year-old John needed in order to successfully run a farm of his own.

If young John died without an heir, his father wrote in his will, everything John inherited would become his brother Isaac's. The desire to keep land in the hands of male heirs was strong throughout Little Compton, and the Baileys were no exception. If the younger John married but did not have children, his wife could inherit the property. His father's will made sure this would not happen, and that the farm would stay in the Bailey family. The older John also made sure young John had a home with his brother Isaac until he was able to marry. "I do further order my son Isaac to provide for my son John so long as he shall live unmarried meet [meat] drink washing and lodging and I give my son John a privilege of living in my now dwelling house so long as he shall live unmarried." It was Isaac's wife Sarah who would have borne the brunt of the work created by an extra member of the household.

In John Senior's will the brothers were to share their father's farming and carpentry tools as well as the privilege of gathering seaweed from the shore for fertilizer at what is now Philippi's Beach. Both John's will and inventory show the importance of cloth to the family. Like many of their neighbors the Baileys were clearly manufacturing linen and woolen cloth. This too would have been the work of Sarah and any other women in the household. The family's belongings, as described in John's probate inventory, include a desk, "Chinese cups," items made of silver, books, a couch

Captain John Bailey's Farm as it appeared to Sydney Burleigh around 1900.
Painting by Sydney Burleigh. Courtesy of Fred Bridge.

bed, window curtains and a chair carriage. All of these items indicate a level of comfort, modernity and refinement within the Bailey home. Their livestock included primarily sheep (65) and pigs (18). Though like almost every Little Compton family they also owned cows, and like other wealthy families, horses (3).

The mention of powder, powder horns, lead balls, a gun, a bayonet and a sword in the probate inventory is a reminder that the American Revolution was in full swing around them. Guns and swords are frequently listed in inventories, but powder and ammunition seldom appear. The Baileys must have had a large enough quantity to attract the attention of the inventory takers.[8] According to Benjamin Franklin Wilbour, young John served in the Revolution eventually achieving the rank of Captain. His father would be very pleased that he survived the war and married his second cousin Lydia Bailey in 1781. Young John and Lydia produced a dozen heirs including a set of twins, but none of these children ever inherited a portion of their grandfather's farm. John sold his farm to his brother Isaac in 1803 for $5,300.[9] It is not clear where John and his family lived next, but they remained in Little Compton. Lydia died four years later at the age of forty-seven. Her youngest child was five years old at the time.

Isaac Bailey (1742–1813) &
Sarah Manchester (1753–1828)

Isaac Bailey was now the owner of three adjacent farms: his father's homestead farm on which Isaac and his family lived, his brother John's farm to the north and the White Farm to the south which he purchased back from Oliver White's five children in 1792.[10] The White children, who appeared to be Quakers, had scattered throughout Southern New England. The small pieces of their father's farm they each inherited held no value to them beyond the prices they could bring.

Isaac on the other hand was well positioned to provide each of his three sons a fine Little Compton farm of his own. When contemplating his death in 1813 Isaac wrote, "esteeming it is my Indeffensable Duty to Set my house in order before I die I do make this my last will and testament."[11] Isaac did indeed set "his house in order" leaving his sons paragraphs of detailed instructions concerning the care of their mother Sarah, their widowed sister Mary Bailey Richmond and the distribution of Isaac's belongings, both real estate and personal property. His will also begins to paint a picture of the family home by listing some of its rooms and out-buildings. "I give to my well beloved and affectionate wife Sarah Bailey all the chambers and rooms above stairs excepting two bedrooms at the head of the kitchen stairs and the garret – also a privilege in the garret cellar washhouse and other outbuildings to improve as long as she remain my widow." Based on these few lines we learn that the Bailey House was a large two-story building with a garret or attic above and at least two sets of stairs. The second floor appears to have held numerous rooms.

Isaac ordered in his will that his three sons share the responsibility of providing for their mother and detailed a list of supplies that she was to receive each year. The list shows us the provisions a well-to-do woman was expected to have at the beginning of the nineteenth century. His daughter Mary received similar provisions to be provided by her brothers, though her quantities were approximately halved.

- *300 weight of pork*
- *300 weight of beef "they to find tubs and cut and salt her meat at their expense"*
- *20 bushels of indian meal*
- *Four bushels of rye meal,*
- *Two barrels of flour*
- *Half a bushel of salt*
- *150 weight of cheese*
- *50 weight of butter*
- *Thirty weight of tried tallow*
- *And twenty weight of hogs fat*
- *Thirty weight of sugar*
- *Nine gallons of molasses*
- *Two barrels of cider,*
- *Fifteen bushels of winter apples*
- *One bushel of quinces and all kinds of summer fruit*
- *Sauce and vinegar that she may need*
- *Six pound of tea*

- *Eight pound of coffee*
- *Three pound of chocklate*
- *Also to be provided by my two youngest sons Tillinghast and Peleg forty weight of flax and twenty weight of good fine wool yearly*
- *Also to be provided by three sons $50 yearly and five cords and one half of wood if she need, it to be prepared for the fire*
- *Also Abraham to provide as much milk and cream as she may need*
- *I also request that my sons remember my widow with regard to fresh meat poultry and eggs.*

In return for following their father's wishes all three sons received a farm. Abraham inherited the ninety-acre homestead farm in the center of the property. Peleg received the forty-acre farm to the north, and Tilling-hast was given the White Farm to the south.

Each of the farms included salt meadow, which was a valuable source of hay, as well as the right to collect seaweed for fertilizer on what is now Philippi's Beach. The brothers were to share Isaac's woodlots in the Cole-brook area. Many if not most Little Compton farmers owned woodlots some distance from their farm and often in Colebrook woods. Firewood

Horse Sheds on the Commons, c. 1910. Postcard by O.E. Dubois. LCHS Collection.

was their only source of heat and was critical to their survival. Teams of men would visit the woodlots at least once a year, often camping there until they cut a sufficient supply to bring home. The three men also shared their father's shed on the Commons, a dry place to tie up their horses during Sunday's long church services.

Isaac's four daughters received $500 each and some personal items. Previously, the girls would have been given a dowry when they married consisting of valuable household goods, most especially a featherbed. Isaac also gave a special gift of cash to just one of his grandchildren, his name-sake Isaac Bailey Richmond, his daughter Mary's son. In 1812 after the early death of her husband Joshua Richmond, a prosperous Providence merchant, Mary and her six children came home to Little Compton to live with her parents. Isaac, her oldest child, grew to love the family farm and would one day buy it for himself.

In 1813 just before Isaac Bailey's death at the age of seventy-one the Bailey homestead appears to have included at least twenty people: Isaac and his wife Sarah Manchester; their daughter Mary and her six children; their son Deacon Abraham Bailey, his wife Anna Chase and the first nine of their fourteen children; as well as any live-in servants they would have employed.[12] The Bailey's were well-to-do, but their large home was not just a show of wealth; it was a necessity for an expanding family.

Please see page 78 to continue the History of the Deacon Abraham Bailey Farm and the Seaconnet House.

Please see page 88 for the history of the Tillinghast Bailey Farm and the Marsh House.

Please see page 100 for the history of the Peleg Bailey Farm and the Lunt House.

The Seaconnet House. Photo by Bart Brownell.

The Seaconnet House

FROM GRAND HOTEL TO OFFICERS' QUARTERS

By Marjory O'Toole

A large two-story house with a Victorian flair, Seaconnet House is remarkable for its unconventional use at two points in its history; first as the site of an astonishingly large hotel prior to the Civil War and second as quarters for Fort Church's officers during World War II.

The land on which the house sits passed through four generations of Bailey's before Deacon Abraham Bailey inherited it from his father Isaac in 1813. Isaac was the definition of a family patriarch – repurchasing land that once belonged to his ancestors, providing farms for three of his sons and guaranteeing the care of his widowed daughter and six grandchildren even after his death.

Abraham Bailey (1772–1835) & Anna Chase (1777–1841)

Sadly, Deacon Abraham Bailey did not enjoy the long prosperous life his father did. During his lifetime, the Deacon and his large family lived very comfortably, though they suffered the early deaths of four of their fourteen children. The family grew corn and potatoes, raised sheep, and wove their wool into fabric on their family loom. They owned six horse-drawn vehicles including a comfortable chaise and two sleighs. Their home and farm were filled with modern conveniences like a cast iron stove, a "washing machine" and a "corn machine," (Both machines were hand-operated.), as well as luxuries like thirty books, a clock and silver spoons. The most expensive item Abraham owned was his pew in the Congregational meeting house valued at $99, but when he died at the age of sixty-four, Abraham left his wife and children deeply in debt.[1]

Abraham owed over $4,000 to fifty-five different men, women and organizations when he passed away in 1835. His greatest debt, $1,500, was to his son Pardon who served as his executor. The Little Compton Probate Court declared the estate insolvent, and gave Pardon permission to sell everything except his mother Anna's allowance due to her as a widow. At a series of auctions lasting a day and a half, Peleg sold all of Abraham's personal belongings, his livestock, vehicles and farm. When the debts were paid his heirs were left with just over $1,460 to be divided into thirteen shares. Each share was $112. The Bailey Farm was sold, but not too far out of the family.

Ezra Coe (1787–1851) &
* Deborah Bailey Earle Bartlett (1780–1853)*
Joseph Coe (1813–1886) &
* Julia Ann Taylor (1811–1875)*

Abraham's indebtedness ended the simple father to son inheritance that this portion of the Bailey farm had experienced so far, but Abraham's homestead farm still stayed within the extended family. When the auction or "public Vendee" was held at Abraham's house on January 16, 1837 the highest bidders were Ezra Coe and his son Joseph.[2] Ezra was Abraham's brother-in-law, and Joseph was his nephew. Ezra had married two of Abraham's sisters, first Mary and later Deborah. Deborah Bailey Earle Barrett Coe was already a two-time widow when she married Ezra at the age of thirty-eight. Joseph was Mary's oldest son. Ezra & Joseph's purchase of the farm that was once Deborah's childhood home must have been a very important moment for her.

The Coes had big plans. Together they paid $7,500 for the property, $4,000 of which they borrowed. Not only were they going to be farmers, they were going to be hotel operators. With Joseph in the lead and Ezra essentially a silent partner, the Coes transformed Deacon Bailey's farm into a guest house, and in the winter of 1845-46 they undertook an enormous expansion to create a surprisingly large and very early hotel, the first in Little Compton. They called their hotel "Seaconnet House" and aggressively advertised it in the New York papers.

Seaconnet House. LCHS Collection.

The advertisement read:

WATERING PLACE – Seaconnet House, Seaconnet Point Little Compton, R.I. – The subscriber begs leave to inform the public, that this pleasantly situated house will be opened and ready to receive company on the 15th June. Large additions have been made to the house and outbuildings during the last Winter and Spring – good and experienced help in all the several departments are secured, and no exertions on his part shall be wanting to make this one of the pleasantest Summer resorts in the country.

Sea-bathing within three-quarters of a mile. Conveyance to and from at all hours of the day.

Gentlemen fond of fishing or fowling will find this place very much to their mind.

A stage will leave the house daily at 8 A.M. and arrive at Fall River in season for the 3 o'clock steamer for Providence; also in season for the 3½ o'clock train of cars for Boston. Returning, leaves Fall River at 1 P.M. and arrives at 4 P.M.

A stage now runs alternative days for New-Bedford leaving the house at 8 A.M. and returning the next day after the arrive of the morning train from Boston. After the first of July it will run daily, leaving the Seaconnet House at 7½ A.M. and New-Bedford at ½ before 2 P.M.; these lines also intersect at Stone Bridge with the daily stage for Newport.

JOSEPH COE
Little Compton, R.I. June 5, 1846[3]

Billed as both a seaside resort and a sporting lodge, the Coes had high hopes for their new venture. This was the first large scale effort to promote Little Compton as a summer community to the public, and it would not be repeated until well after the Civil War during the steamship era.

Seaconnet House may not have lived up to Joseph's expectations. Just three years later Joseph focused on what he believed to be an even greater money-making scheme – The California Gold Rush. Now acting without his father, Joseph mortgaged Seaconnet House to his first cousin Isaac Bailey Richmond, the fatherless boy who had grown up on the property when it was his grandfather Isaac Bailey's house. Joseph received $18,000 from Isaac in January of 1849, and by February he sailed out of New Bedford on the ship *William and Henry* bound for California with his brother Jethro.[4] The Coe brothers were among the approximately twenty-five Little Compton men who tried to make their fortune in the Gold Rush. Like most of them, the Coes did not succeed. By April Joseph had failed to pay Isaac the $12,000 plus interest required by the mortgage, and tragically by October Jethro was dead.

Isaac Bailey Richmond (1798–1888) &
Abigail Brown (1803–1884)

As stipulated by their agreement Isaac B. Richmond took control of the property and sold it at public auction to recover his investment. Isaac was the high bidder. He acquired the property in 1853 for $5 plus the money he had advanced Joseph.[5] Isaac now owned his grandfather's property and a giant hotel.

Isaac's own son Henry I. Richmond was in Benica, California at this time. It is likely that he went in 1849 in conjunction with his cousins the Coes. Isaac may have used his new purchase to lure his son back to the safety of Little Compton. In 1854 Isaac sold Henry "Seaconnett Farm" for $7,000. In addition to the $7000, Henry paid his mother Abigail one dollar to sign away her "rights of dower and power of thirds."[6] Widows at the time were entitled to one third of their husband's property, the rest went to his children or other heirs.

Isaac B. Richmond. LCHS Collection.

Henry Richmond (1824–1899) &
Frances Ellen Palmer (1831–1896)

Like many men of his generation Henry had no intention of becoming a farmer. He had been a merchant in California in partnership with his brother Preston, but the venture was short lived. By the mid-1850s both men were back in New England. Henry married a Boston girl Frances Ellen Palmer in 1859. The couple had just one child, Henry Junior. Small families were a trend in late-nineteenth-century Little Compton.

Either Henry or his designee continued to run the Seaconnet House as a hotel until approximately 1860. *The New Bedford Standard* reported in September 1863:

The Seaconet House, situated at Seconet Point, Little Compton is being taken down having been closed for the past two or three season, for lack of patronage.[7]

The Richmonds maintained ownership of the property, rebuilding a graceful summer home on the site of the hotel. During the off-season the family lived in Boston. Henry was involved in the South American and Manila trade and managed to retire before he was fifty-five. The 1880 Federal Census shows Henry, Frances and Henry Junior living in Mrs. Eliza Hayes' Boarding House on Holyoke Street in Boston. Henry was listed a retired merchant, Frances was "at home" and fourteen-year-old Henry Junior was at school.[8]

The Seaconnet House we see today is much like the house created by Henry and Frances Richmond around 1863. One of the home's finest features is its "Dancing Staircase" leading to the second floor. When the Richmonds were in Little Compton they were part of a tight knit social circle that included their neighbors and cousins – the Baileys. Sarah Soule Wilbour a local diarist recorded her visits with them all, as well as the parties they attended throughout the late 1880s. Once Sarah had a visit from "young Mister Richmond" (Henry Junior) whom she recorded as a "very nice boy."[9]

Harry Richmond (1865-1956)

Henry Isaac Richmond's 1922 Passport Photo.

When the elder Henry died in 1899 the property passed to Henry Junior, better known as Harry. Harry Richmond never married and enjoyed a bachelor's life filled with international travel, even voyaging as far as Japan in 1913.[10] While Harry was traveling, caretaker Joseph Pacheco kept a watchful eye on the property living in a cottage at the rear of the estate.[11] Harry's cousin Joshua Richmond recalled seeing him often "on his bike in puttees and white linen jodhpurs…with a drooping "Fu Manchu" mustache."[12] Josh also noted that Harry's farm was the site of three holes of golf and a tennis court created as the forerunner of the Sakonnet Golf Club.[13] Seaconnet Farm was Harry's home base for many years both before and after World War II intervened.

SEIZED BY EMINENT DOMAIN

In 1943 as the United States Army was turning the southwest corner of Little Compton into a sprawling military base, they seized Harry Richmond's home and the acreage surrounding it to use as officers' quarters. The General Services Administration paid Harry $15,940 for the property.[14] Many other historic buildings in the area were also seized. Some like the Peleg Bailey House were used for barracks, while others like the Daniel Wilbor House were destroyed. The large size, the elegance and the relatively new construction of the Seaconnet House saved it from demolition.

The home's current owner James "Shay" Lynch reports, "The Army did make some 'improvements,' including an addition with eleven urinals. They used the house not only to house officers but also to entertain. The first floor of the house was often used for dances including one that hosted military officers from Brazil in full dress uniforms and white gloves dancing the tango to the delight of the local women.[15]

The Army also built a small administration building in the front yard. Like all of Fort Church's new buildings it was designed to look like an ordinary farm building from a distance. This was an effort to keep the true extent and fire power of Fort Church secret from the enemy. This building was sold in 1955 and moved to the northeast to be repurposed as part of the Lunt House.[16]

A RICHMOND HOME AGAIN

At the end of the war the fort was closed, and the General Services Administration set about selling the seized properties. Most were sold by lottery, and there was no guarantee original owners would regain their homes. Harry Richmond was fortunate. He was able to repurchase his home and the 5.6 acres around it in 1950 for $23,000 prior to the lotteries taking place.[17] Harry had to promise that the property would be for personal use, not for development, for at least two years. At the same time Carson Feibiger of Essex, MA purchased twenty-two acres of Harry's old property from the government for $15,000 and made the same promise. Almost two years to the date of purchase Feibiger sold the property back to Richmond for "$10 and other valuable considerations."[18] Like his great-great-grandfather Isaac Bailey, Harry was pulling the family farm back together.

Unfortunately, he did not get to enjoy it for long. Toward the end of his life Harry struggled with mental health issues and lived his last few years at Butler Hospital in Providence. He passed away in 1956. According to family stories, Harry had his tombstone installed at the base of the Dancing Staircase.[19] A year after his death Harry's administrators sold over 100 acres of his land, which stretched across both sides of Warren's Point Road, to Richmond Properties, Inc. an association of Harry's family members.[20]

Cousin Joshua Richmond took ownership of Seaconnet House and the four plus acres around it in 1960. He and his family enjoyed it as their summer home and added a sun room to the east on the foundation of an old wing. The room was designed by Little Compton architect Tom Marvell, and the roof is meant to look like the hull of a boat. In 1973 Josh and Gerry Richmond and their children moved into another historic family home, the Isaac Bailey Richmond House on South of the Commons. Shay Lynch has owned the property he calls "The Palace" since that time, making small changes and improvements as his family's needs changed. In 2014 he added a bedroom addition to the north and had heat installed on the second floor.

One of the home's most interesting outdoor features is the "HaHa," a beautiful sunken garden surrounded by the tall stone walls that once served as the basement for an addition. The Army had installed a large military kitchen in the addition, and Josh and Gerry Richmond took it down.[21] On a clear day visitors to the HaHa can see Martha's Vineyard in the distance. Beyond the HaHa is the Hen House cottage that now has two bedrooms and a bath.

The changing use of the Seaconnet House reflects major shifts in Little Compton's town-wide history. At first a farmhouse like every other home in Little Compton, it transitioned into the town's first summer hotel, an early summer home, military housing during the upheaval of World War II and then back to a present-day summer home. It is both a beautiful historic property and a testament to the ability of Little Compton's people and properties to prosper and persist as they adapt and change over time.

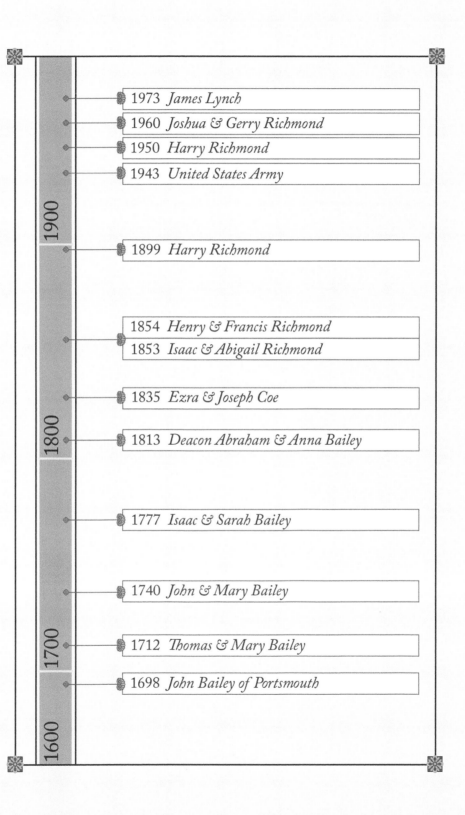

1973 *James Lynch*

1960 *Joshua & Gerry Richmond*

1950 *Harry Richmond*

1943 *United States Army*

1900

1899 *Harry Richmond*

1854 *Henry & Francis Richmond*

1853 *Isaac & Abigail Richmond*

1835 *Ezra & Joseph Coe*

1813 *Deacon Abraham & Anna Bailey*

1800

1777 *Isaac & Sarah Bailey*

1740 *John & Mary Bailey*

1712 *Thomas & Mary Bailey*

1700

1698 *John Bailey of Portsmouth*

1600

The Marsh House. Photo by Bart Brownell.

The Marsh House

A BEACH CLUB REINVENTED

By Marjory O'Toole

Tillinghast Bailey (1783–1852) &
Anna Briggs (1782–post-1850)

Tillinghast Bailey inherited "The White Farm" at his father Isaac's death in 1813. The 115-acre farm stretched across both sides of Warren's Point Road. It was bounded to the north by his brother Abraham's farm, to the south by the Warren's Point farms of his Bailey-Grinnell cousins, to the west by Long Pond, and to the east by what was then known as the "Beach to Brigg's Creek" and today is Philippi's Beach. The beach was an important part of the farm providing essential access to seaweed that Tillinghast and his brothers Abraham and Peleg used to fertilize their fields.

Local beaches were not yet a source of entertainment except for farm boys who might take a quick dip on a hot summer day. Over the course of the next one hundred years that would change dramatically. Little Compton's beaches would become magnets for thousands of city-dwellers on summer holiday. The Depression-era owners of Philippi's Beach tried to attract their share of the summer crowd, but they did not succeed.

Tillinghast and his wife Anna had five boys and two girls born between 1805 and 1816. Their oldest was Sarah Ann. In an unusual twist on the standard Little Compton custom, it was Sarah and not her brothers who became the next owner of the Tillinghast Bailey Farm.

Lemuel Sisson, Senior (1769–1849)
David Sisson (1803–1874) &
Sarah Bailey Sisson (1805–1895)

Sarah married her Sakonnet Point neighbor David Sisson around 1827. David was one of Lemuel Sisson's thirteen children. Lemuel and his clan arrived in Sakonnet Point in 1816 as the caretakers of the huge Rotch Farm at Sakonnet Point. The family brought their Methodist faith with them. Lemuel started the town's first Methodist meetings at his home in 1820. The religion appealed to Little Compton's families, and over time the congregation built three different churches, each one significantly larger than the last.

Lemuel Sisson Senior, 1769-1849.
LCHS Collection.

In 1830 David and his father Lemuel pooled their resources and purchased Tillinghast Bailey's house and farm for $6,000. Forty-seven-year-old Tillinghast referred to himself as a "merchant" in the deed, a sign that his farming days were over.[1] By 1830 Tillinghast had already moved his family to the bustling port city of New Bedford to pursue business rather than agriculture. He and his wife Anna lived the rest of their lives surrounded by the elegant sea captains' homes of New Bedford.[2] The deed listed Lemuel as a Little Compton yeoman, a property owner who farmed his own land, and David as a Troy (Fall River) gentleman, a property owner who did not do physical labor.

Because of her husband's purchase Sarah was now part-owner of her Bailey family farm, but it is doubtful she ever lived there as a married woman. David was a serious and successful businessman. He moved his family from Fall River to Cranston to Providence always building his business ventures. The couple lost their first child William when he was a little over a year old. Their second child Henry Tillinghast Sisson was born in 1831 and grew up to be a Civil War hero and the inventor of the loose-leaf binder.

The 1830 census shows David's brother Lemuel Junior living on the Tillinghast Bailey Farm with his wife Comfort Simmons. Their first child was born a little later that year. The family was still there in 1850, now with two teenage daughters and Comfort's mother Nancy. Several of Lemuel's brothers lived nearby, undoubtedly joining forces whenever their farming chores required extra hands.

Lemuel Senior passed away in 1849 and left no will. His portion of the White Farm passed in even shares to each of his children. In 1853 all of David's brothers and sisters, including Lemuel Junior, signed their shares of "The White Farm" over to David in exchange for $3,500 making David the sole owner of the Tillinghast Bailey Farm.[3] Census records indicated that Lemuel Junior continued to live on the farm through 1860.[4]

By 1870 Lemuel Junior had retired, and he and Comfort moved closer to her Simmons family members on Sakonnet Point Road. They occupied a two-family home now known as the Bailey-Sisson House. Their widowed daughter Mary Tallman and her two children lived with them on one side of the house, and their other daughter Susan lived on the other side of the house with her husband Edwin Seabury, a farmer and brother to Albert Seabury.[5] Susan and Edwin shared their side of the house with a farmhand and an Irish maid, Margaret Donnelly. Margaret could neither read nor write, but she moved from Ireland to try to make a better life for herself. She was one of many Irish immigrants working for Little Compton families at the time.[6]

In 1854 David Sisson completed work on the Stone House, an impressive stone mansion at Sakonnet Point, truly the finest home in Little Compton. It was located on the Rotch Farm which he bought from his brother Lemuel. According to Benjamin Franklin Wilbour the

The Bailey-Sisson House, c. 1910. Postcard by O.E. Dubois. LCHS Collection.

Sissons used the leftover stones from the construction of the first Sakonnet Harbor breakwater to build their home.[7] The Sissons were full-time Little Compton residents by 1860. At that time David headed a household of fourteen people at the Stone House including eight farm laborers and servants.[8]

Henry (1842–1892) & Sarah Bundy (1865–1932)

David and his brother Lemuel passed away in February 1874 within days of each other. All of David's properties passed to his only son Colonel Henry T. Sisson.[9] Of all the men interested in developing Sakonnet Point into a summer colony Henry Sisson was the most ambitious, but instead of dividing his Warren's Point property into small house lots, as he later tried to do with the Rotch Farm, he sold the entire 115-acre Tillinghast Bailey Farm to Henry and Sarah Bundy of Cumberland, Rhode Island for "one dollar and other valuable considerations" in 1878.[10]

The Bundy Farm. LCHS Collection.

Henry Bundy was a fellow Civil War Veteran. At the time he signed the deed with Colonel Sisson, Bundy also took out a $4,000 mortgage. Over the years many Little Compton properties have been sold for very small amounts on paper while more substantial amounts changed hands privately.

The Bundys built an impressive home and offered room and board to summer guests.[11] This type of guest house flourished throughout Little Compton around the turn-of-the-last-century and in general was much more successful than Joseph Coe's attempt with the very large "Seaconnet House" hotel on the abutting farm in the 1840s.[12] The Bundys had four children. Their youngest son Richard became a dentist and, after spending some time in Providence, lived with his family in Henry Sisson's Stone House in the 1950s.

John McGowan (1851–1917) & Eva McGowan (1862–1931)

In 1909 the widow Sarah Bundy sold the entire property to John and Eva McGowan for the token sum of $10. The deed still included the farm's woodlot in the "Cold-Brook Wood."[13] The McGowan's had a modern survey of the property done just prior to signing the deed. The farm included 140 acres, 52.5 acres were mowed or cultivated, 36 acres were pasture land and 51 acres were marsh or unusable land. The plan shows the location of the stone walls dividing the various meadows and pastures and provides us with a glimpse at the way the farm was organized by Tillinghast Bailey and his ancestors.

The McGowans lived in the Bundy House for several years and then built a much grander house known as "Sealands" on the southern portion of their property. The Bundy's house was moved to the west side of Warren's Point Road where it became the home of Wallace Dempster and was called the "Taj Mahal."[14] It has since been demolished. Eva McGowan was very involved in the local Episcopal Church and donated the funds to build a rectory next to the Sakonnet Point location of St. Andrew's by the Sea in 1933.[15]

Dr. Philemon Truesdale (1874–1945) &
Minna Dickenson Truesdale

In 1924 the widowed Mrs. McGowan deeded the north portion of her property to Doctor Philemon E. Truesdale. The parcel was roughly forty acres of land that stretched from Henry Richmond's farm to the north to just south of the laneway to the beach. Mrs. McGowan kept the southern portion of her property containing Sealands for herself and reserved the right to cross over the Truesdale's property one week each year for gathering seaweed.[16] The doctor and his wife Minna agreed to pay Mrs. McGowan $7,500 over the course of five years plus interest for the property.[17]

Dr. Philemon E. Truesdale.
Courtesy of the Philippi Family.

After they paid off the mortgage in 1928 the Truesdales immediately deeded Daphne Withington of Norfolk, Massachusetts two lots of land totaling just under three acres. Soon they sold an oceanfront lot to the Reverend Henry Medary and wife Amie for $1.[18] For the first time these deeds included a right of way to the beach for swimming and bathing rather than gathering seaweed.

Later in 1928 the Truesdales had plans drawn for a development they called "Sea Acres." The focal point of the development was a "Bathing Beach," and the cart path used to collect seaweed was slightly rerouted and rechristened "Beach Street." The Truesdales and their Beach Street neighbors joined together in 1929 to give the utility companies permission to provide electricity and telephone service to their homes.[19]

An often repeated family story says that Doctor Truesdale acquired this particular piece of property because he performed his "upside down stomach surgery" on a grateful patient who found it easier to pay with land than with cash.[20] The Truesdale's mortgage to Mrs. McGowan makes that particular story unlikely, but it is quite true that Doctor Truesdale pioneered a surgical technique to repair diaphragmatic hernias or

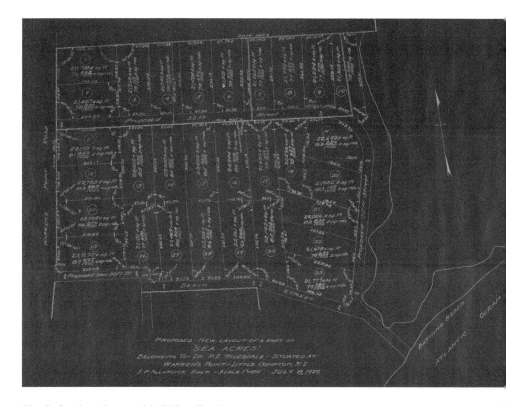

Plan for Sea Acres. Courtesy of the Philippi Family.

"upside-down-stomachs." In 1935 a ten-year-old girl from Omaha, Nebraska traveled to Fall River to the Truesdale Hospital to receive the surgery. Alice McHenry's hometown raised money for her trip, and the doctor performed the operation for free. Both Alice and Doctor Truesdale became media darlings.

Doctor Truesdale believed in acquiring property. He owned waterfront farms all along the coast including Goosewing Farm and Westport Point. The doctor wanted to farm to ensure that his patients at the hospital had nutritious food during the Depression and World War II. He was also a sportsman. The Tillinghast Bailey Farm was especially appealing because of its proximity to Briggs' Marsh, an excellent spot for fishing and duck hunting. The property included "East Island" in Briggs' Marsh which was equipped with a small duck hunting camp house. A wooden boardwalk led the way across the marsh to the camp.[21]

Doctor Truesdale and his family hoped that his new Bathing Beach would attract visitors, and they built a substantial beach club much like the one on Warren's Point. The club never really took off. There were two summers of thick red seaweed that discouraged swimmers. The beach itself was a cobblestone beach without much sand, certainly a factor that contributed to the club's lack of success.[22] Randy Byers remembers that

Doctor Truesdale's club was not very popular because the summer people did not like to walk that far. Not to mention that it opened just as America's Great Depression was underway. By 1937 the club was closed to the public, but the Truesdale family put the buildings to good use.

The Beach Club in its original location. Courtesy of the Philippi Family.

Alexander Philippi & Elizabeth Philippi

Doctor and Mrs. Truesdale gave the club buildings and a half acre of land on Beach Street to their daughter Elizabeth and her husband Alexander Philippi. The couple moved the buildings off the beach and into

their current location in the spring of 1938. The timing could not have been better.

That September the devastating 1938 Hurricane swept along Little Compton's shoreline leaving a wake of devastation in its path. The club house buildings survived in their new location, though ocean water surged beneath them. The hurricane dramatically altered Brigg's Marsh, flooding acres and acres of land that were once used as salt-

The Marsh House just after its move from the beach. Courtesy of the Philippi family.

marsh meadows and bringing tons of sand up onto what is now called Philippi's Beach.

The Philippi's christened their new summer home Marsh House. Alexander worked in the family business, the American Thread Company. He and Elizabeth and their five children moved from New Jersey to Kentucky before eventually settling in Little Compton as year-round residents in the 1940s. The center portion of the Marsh House, called the summer living room, was the beach club's central area complete with a hardwood floor for dancing and a massive beach stone fireplace. The room was moved with the fireplace intact. The stones were collected right on Philippi's Beach, and a half model of Doctor Truesdale's sailboat *Twilight* is embedded in its face. The north and south wings of the house are the repurposed bath house buildings. They were used "as is" with exterior shingles applied right over the line of bathhouse doors. The north wing, containing bedrooms, and the summer living room have never been heated. The heated south wing contains additional bedrooms, a kitchen and a winter living room.

Alexander and Elizabeth (Libby) Philippi.
Courtesy of the Philippi Family.

Marsh House has a long history as a social hub for the extended Truesdale family and Little Compton's summer community.[23] For decades its "Derby Day" and "Day After Thanksgiving" Parties were the unofficial beginning and end of the social season in Little Compton. The Marsh House parties started in the 1940s and several of them continue to this day.

The first Saturday in May signals the annual Kentucky Derby Party, a nod to the time the Philippi family spent living in Kentucky. As many as a hundred people attend, bringing hors d'oeuvres and taking part in some good-natured betting. Each year the

Cartoon by Walter Cluett. Courtesy of the Philippi Family.

Marsh House is also the site of the Truesdale family Thanksgiving with up to seventy people attending. The family lights the fireplace the day before to give the large room time to warm up. The Day-After Party became so large it was disbanded about a decade ago.

In the past the family also celebrated Christmas at the house and would just shut the door to the unheated central room when the holiday was over. They would enter again at Easter, and the Easter Bunny would leave the children's baskets under the still-green Christmas tree.[24]

The family ran a children's camp on the property in the 1960s operated

Thanksgiving, 1977. Courtesy of the Philippi Family.

by their daughter Dale. Little Compton's grandparents were happy their little ones had a place to go and burn off some steam. The camp had a reputation for being "tough." The garage served as camp headquarters. One day Minnie the family dog ate every camper's lunch. Dale quickly made seventeen peanut-butter-and-jelly sandwiches.[25]

Elizabeth Philippi Millikin

The Philippis left the Marsh House to their children as tenants in common. Through the years Elizabeth "Bunny" Philippi Millikin has become the sole owner. The house is still enjoyed each summer by an ever-growing extended family. Over time the house's lot also grew from one half to almost three acres. Porches and patios have been added and extended through the years providing stunning water views. Signs of the home's beach club origins are still visible throughout the house. The summer living room is an elegant gathering place with its imposing stone fireplace and its dark paneled walls while the long rows of bathhouse bedrooms epitomize casual summer days on the beach.

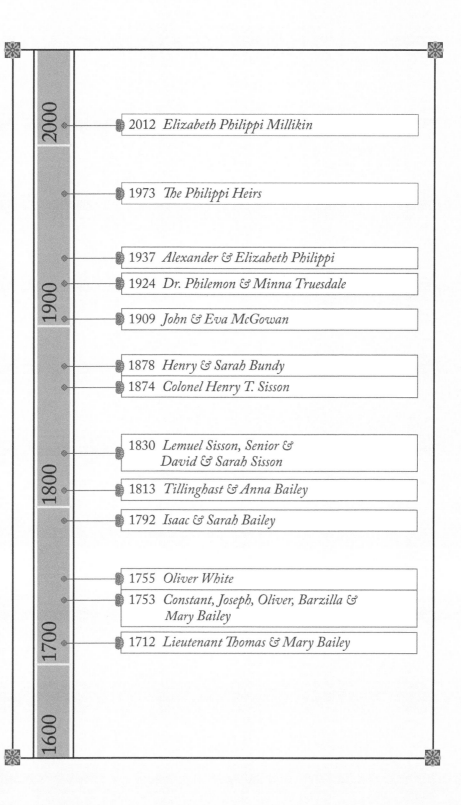

2012 *Elizabeth Philippi Millikin*

1973 *The Philippi Heirs*

1937 *Alexander & Elizabeth Philippi*

1924 *Dr. Philemon & Minna Truesdale*

1909 *John & Eva McGowan*

1878 *Henry & Sarah Bundy*

1874 *Colonel Henry T. Sisson*

1830 *Lemuel Sisson, Senior &*
David & Sarah Sisson

1813 *Tillinghast & Anna Bailey*

1792 *Isaac & Sarah Bailey*

1755 *Oliver White*

1753 *Constant, Joseph, Oliver, Barzilla &*
Mary Bailey

1712 *Lieutenant Thomas & Mary Bailey*

2000

1900

1800

1700

1600

The Lunt House. Photo by Bart Brownell.

The Lunt House

THE PELEG BAILEY FARM

By Piper Hawes

The story of the Lunt House is the story of Little Compton writ small. Its history encompasses many of the key elements of the town's history. The story begins with the Sakonnets, the local Native American inhabitants of the land and continues with the arrival of the first European colonists.

The land on which the house sits is part of a larger tract purchased from the Sakonnets by Little Compton's first English Proprietors in 1675. The Proprietors distributed the land by lottery among themselves. This particular parcel overlooking Briggs Marsh remained unchanged for hundreds of years. It was farmed until the outbreak of World War II, when it and the surrounding areas were taken by the US Army to become part of the East Reservation of Fort Church. For the first time the land had a building – a barracks disguised to look like a summer cottage from the air.

When the war ended, the fort was declared unneeded for military purposes. The land was sold to the highest bidder by silent auction. Here the story comes full circle. The land was purchased by a consortium made up of some of the descendants of the original Proprietors, as well as their Warren's Point neighbors, who then distributed lots among members and friends.

This particular lot had a succession of owners who came for the summer and transformed two military buildings first into a real summer cottage and then into a year-round home.

Peleg Bailey (1788–1860) & Sarah Gray (1783–1865)

When Isaac Bailey died in 1813 his holdings were divided into three farms for his three sons. The eldest, Abraham inherited the homestead farm at the center, Tillinghast inherited the White Farm to the south by Philippi's Beach, and his youngest son, Peleg, inherited the northern farm, afterwards known as the "Peleg Bailey Farm."

The farm is largely made up of two eighteen-acre lots, Number 1 and Number 4, drawn in the Proprietor's lottery of 1675. The original owners, John Pinson and Simon Rouse, like many of their fellow Plymouth Colony proprietors, sold their Little Compton lots relatively quickly. By 1690 these thirty-six acres were owned by Nathaniel Warren who in turn sold them to John Bailey in 1697.[1]

Isaac Bailey's will delineated his son Peleg's land *"...as the land I bought of my brother John Bailey, with all buildings and also pasture to westward and northward of the highway on my homestead farm. And all the land I bought of the Widow Head and also salt meadow of my homestead farm."*[2]

Peleg Bailey married Sarah Gray in 1810. Their only child Caroline was born a year later. Rather than live in his father's crowded home, Peleg and Sarah moved into his Uncle John's old house on the northernmost of three adjacent family farms. Three years later upon his father's death, the house

Sarah Bailey's Tea Set. A gift to the LCHS by her descendants, the Bartlett Family, in 2014.

and farm officially became his. Peleg's small family was often joined by "hired boys" who lived with him and helped farm the land. For many years there was a sign in front of the Peleg Bailey Farm announcing "Pigs for Sale." Because the sign was there for so long, locals began referring to the house as such. An early twentieth-century photograph shows that the eighteenth-century house was added to, as needs required, growing into a substantial dwelling.

THE SEAWEED WAR

While his brothers owned the two farms to the south Peleg was able to fertilize his farm with seaweed gathered from his brother Tillinghast's beach. Their father's will made sure that all three sons were able to partake

The Peleg Bailey Farmhouse, c. 1910. LCHS Collection.

of the seaweed privilege. Over time both farms were sold to men who had married Bailey women, and then the squabbling began.

In 1849 Peleg Bailey and Joseph and Ezra Coe, the new owners of Abraham Bailey's farm, and Lemuel and David Sisson, the new owners of Tillinghast Bailey's White Farm, referred their differences of opinion over the privileges delineated in the will to the Supreme Court of Rhode Island.

Tillinghast's farm had *"an extensive beach, on which sea-weed drifted and lodged."* Isaac Bailey's will had given his two sons — Peleg and Abraham — the right *"to pass and repass to the beach, and there to cart up sea-weed and sand, at any time when they shall see fit, and tip it out in a heap...."* They were to go *"through the pasture we now go, to the north end of the beach meadow, and through that to the Beach."*[3] The court determined that:

- the seaweed privilege was not limited to the lives of Abraham and Peleg
- the plaintiffs had the right to take, cart off and use from the White Beach, seaweed and sand in "proportions corresponding to the respective interests of the parties in the lands"
- the plaintiffs could only pass and repass to the beach the one way as described in Isaac Bailey's will
- the plaintiffs had no right to cut or carry away rockweed, as their right was only limited to *"sea-weed and sea-drift....ordinarily used for manure, which shall float or drift on to the Beach"*
- commissioners be appointed to decide if partition of privilege be by metes and bounds or allotment of time

It would seem that controversy over access to Little Compton's beaches has been part of the town's history from early times.

Peleg farmed in Little Compton for the rest of his life and did well. He invested his earnings in New Bedford-Taunton railroad stock, banks, and real estate in New Bedford. In 1860 he passed away leaving his New Bedford property to his daughter Caroline Bailey Seabury and her daughters. The rest and residue of his estate went to his widow, Sarah.

Gathering Seaweed. LCHS Collection.

FROM FARM TO SUMMER HOME

Sarah soon moved to New Bedford to be near her daughter and granddaughters and sold the farm to John B. Howland in 1863. At the time the farm included sixty acres of upland that stretched across both sides of West Main Road and two acres of saltmarsh.

John Howland died of dysentery at the age of sixty-two and left no will. We learn from a Sheriff's notice posted in the *Newport Mercury* that his son Edward W. Howland inherited the farm, but because of a legal dispute the Sheriff seized the property from Edward, and in 1894 sold it and fifteen other pieces of his property at public auction on the steps of the Little Compton Town Hall. The high bidders were a team of business partners including Town Clerk Frederick R. Brownell, Pardon C. Brownell (for

In 1895 the farm was owned by three investors. Map detail. LCHS Collection.

whom the Brownell Library is named) and George Gray. The sale price of $2,125 for the sixty-acre property was a significant discount from the $8,000 value listed in the 1850 census.

That first summer the partners rented the house to Henry Demarest Lloyd and his family. Lloyd was an investigative journalist with the *Chicago Tribune* and is best known locally as the builder of Watch House at Sakonnet Point, now demolished. The Lloyds would go almost every day by carriage to swim on the beach that would soon bear their name.[4]

In 1901 the three partners sold ten acres of undeveloped land on the west side of the highway to John Flores. Two years later they sold the thirty-five acres of uplands and ten acres of marshland that made up the heart of the Peleg Bailey Farm to Manuel and Rose D'Avila.[5] Both Flores and the D'Avilas were Portuguese immigrants from the Azores representing a new generation of Little Compton farmers.

George Miller and his wife bought the property in 1917.[6] Summer homes were replacing farmhouses in Little Compton, and the Peleg Bailey Farm had new appeal for city dwellers looking for a summer escape.

THE DUNNS

Nine years later the farm and marshland were purchased by Ervin S. Dunn, the son of a mill owner from Woonsocket, Rhode Island.[7] Ervin held various positions in the family business, a worsted wool mill founded in 1895 by his father, John B. Dunn. The elder Dunn was born in Scotland and began working in the woolen and worsted mills there at the tender age of eight. He worked his way through various facets of mill work and was eventually promoted to be the overseer of the weaving department at the Privilege Mill in Woonsocket. He held that position for twenty-one years.

He then started the Dunn Worsted Wool Co., which went from twenty looms to more than two hundred under his tutelage. After his death in 1921 his two sons, Ervin and William, took over the company. The mill thrived at the beginning of the twentieth century when textile mills in the northeast were in their heyday. The Dunn mill provided the army with melton wool and flannel shirting during World War I.

Mrs. Dunn joined the Little Compton Garden Club and the couple settled into the community, but World War II put an end to their summer holidays in Little Compton.[8]

WAR COMES TO LITTLE COMPTON

When Germany invaded Poland in 1939, it became increasingly clear the United States would one day become involved. In preparation for that eventuality, improving our shore defenses suddenly became a high priority. Particularly vulnerable were major harbors and naval installations, which had, at best, outmoded pre-World War I fortifications.

To remedy this, in 1939 the Army began acquiring land in Point Judith and Sakonnet Point for seacoast batteries to protect the naval base at Newport. When France fell to Hitler's Blitzkrieg in 1940 there was concern that Britain might be next, providing Germany with the naval resources to threaten our east coast. Now construction in Little Compton began to accelerate, but as one local remembers, "all this was very hush, hush, confidential, top secret." On May 1, 1940, the War Department named the military establishment at Sakonnet Point the "Fort Church Military Reservation" in honor of town founder Benjamin Church, a leader in King Philip's War, 1675-6.

Fort Church became an integral part of the Army's defense of Narragansett Bay. Land acquisition was ongoing until 1943. Ultimately Fort Church consisted of 217 acres in three separate areas:

- East – The old Peleg Bailey Farm and part of the Seaconnet House Farm - 74 acres,
- West – The Daniel Wilbour Farm running from West Main Road to the Sakonnet River north of the golf course - 122 acres, and
- South – The Lloyd family estate east of Lloyd's Beach - 21 acres.

Each of these parcels housed a pair of large cannons in heavily fortified concrete bunkers with storage and transport for shells that weighed up to one ton each. Some of these could be fired as far as Block Island or Martha's Vineyard.

The guns at Sakonnet Point and Point Judith were linked by underground phone lines to more than a dozen spotting stations, radar installations, and a network of searchlights located on Warren's Point, Gooseberry Neck, Cuttyhunk, Gay Head and Block Island among other sites. PT boats and floating mines provided further protection for the entrances to Narragansett Bay. All of this was linked to a command headquarters buried thirty feet underground on Prudence Island.

The Peleg Bailey Farm, now the "Dunn Farm" was acquired by eminent domain in October 1942.[9] Next door the eight-inch East Reservation gun emplacement was already nearing completion. The District Court of Rhode Island overruled the Dunn family's objections and decreed in October 1942 that, "the United States of America may take immediate possession of the property...to occupy, use and improve." The next year the Army took Henry I. Richmond's Sakonnet House for officers' housing. The officers must have felt this grand house more suitable to their station than the old Peleg Bailey farmhouse and barracks next door. A 1946 photograph of the "Dunn House Barracks" shows the home looking very much as it did in colonial times. After 1947 it was demolished, no doubt considered beyond saving.

Today the Dunn House's colonial barn has become a handsome summerhouse. In its garden, a sunken fieldstone foundation is all that remains of the farmhouse that for nearly 200 years supported Little Compton founding families: Southworths, Richmonds, Baileys, and Howlands.

The Dunn House Barracks, 1946. Courtesy of Walter Bates.

The army didn't waste time using and "improving" the land around the farmhouse. In the East Reservation they built twenty-eight temporary buildings, including a theater, two mess halls, a recreation building, a fire station, an administration building, a supply department and living quarters for the soldiers. These buildings would have to be well heated, well lit, and with indoor plumbing. They would also have to be well constructed, to last a number of years. While the War Department never considered them to be permanent, a 1985 Army inventory showed almost 24,000 World-War-II-era buildings still standing at bases throughout the United States with many still in use.

The Army Corps of Engineers established five principles to guide their building program: speed, simplicity, conservation of materials, flexibility and safety. Standard building plans for wood-frame structures were used. The plans were bundled into construction packages that would have everything needed for a 125-man unit. The battery at East Reservation required a complement of 129 men, but included additional support facilities for the 400 soldiers stationed at the three Reservations.

At Fort Church the standard designs were modified to blend into their New England surroundings and look like typical seaside farms and cottages from the air. On the outside the barracks, mess halls, and related structures shared typical elements including a long rectangular shape, six-over-six double-hung windows, gable roofs and horizontal painted wood siding. One of these barracks masquerading as a cottage was built on what would soon become a real summer home – the Lunt House.

The build-up around Narragansett Bay reached its peak in late 1943, by which time threats to the east coast had become less likely. As the Army had more pressing priorities, manpower at the base was gradually reduced through February 1944.

Although the manning of the Fort Church batteries lasted only about four years, its legacy lived on in Little Compton. Soon after the war, one local resident remembers timing the rounds of a solitary guard, so he and a buddy could sneak into the bunker housing the sixteen-inch guns pointed at Block Island. There one would shimmy out on a cannon barrel. Once in place, his friend would turn on the power and swing the 143-ton barrel around. Shells still stood nearby. Fortunately, a crane was required to move them. Other teenagers in the 1960s found these bunkers attractive party spots – less popular with the neighbors. By the late 1980s South Reservation's bunker had become the basement of a new Haffenreffer house. The bunkers at East and West were filled in and are now overgrown. Their locations are remembered only by the older generation.

THE PROPERTY COMES FULL CIRCLE

Between 1948 and 1954, the General Services Administration (GSA) declared most of the Fort Church properties surplus. The first former owner to reclaim his house was Harry Richmond. He repurchased Sakonnet House for $23,000 in June 1950 and recovered the remaining twenty-two acres two years later.

Then in 1954 the remainder of East Reservation, and all of West and South, were organized for sale. Each of the three bid packages included all the Fort buildings on each reservation. The GSA received a letter of interest from W.B. Dunn, Ervin S. Dunn's brother who hoped to get the property back into the family. By 1954, however, the mill was perhaps on the verge of collapse and money for a land purchase would have been tight. In addition, Dunn's competition was a local partnership of many wealthy members who had pooled their money to submit a combined bid.[10]

The GSA thought a summer auction date would attract wealthy summer residents. Local officials, however, were anxious to get the properties back on the tax rolls and the auction went ahead in April.

The winning bidders were:
- South Reservation to Carl W. Haffenreffer for $35,550 (GSA Estimated Fair Value $49,000).
- West Reservation to Michael Rogers for $42,100. (GSA Estimated Fair Value – Not Listed).

- East Reservation to Sakonnet Properties for $46,315
  (GSA Estimated Fair Value $66,000).

Sakonnet Properties, the consortium of local residents, wasted no time in sub-dividing the old Bailey Farm into fourteen house lots and offering them for sale to members, friends and acquaintances for the purpose of building a new summer community. What happened to the "temporary" structures that were included with the property? In the auction package the government duly noted that an unusual feature of the army buildings was *"the exterior appearance which conforms to that of residential dwellings"*… offering *"ready conversion to that type of use."*

This appealed to many prospective owners at a time when money was scarce. "Use it up, wear it out, make it do, or do without" was an expression popularized during WWII, still appealing to a New Englander's character. It certainly described what happened to many of the WWII buildings on East Reservation, where seventy years later six Fort Church properties continue to provide happy summer memories.

A SUMMER COTTAGE

In October 1954, Zoe and J. Norrish Thorne of Mt. Kisco, New York purchased four and a half acres from Sakonnet Properties. Norrish was a noted art collector and Zoe's passion was breeding Weimaraners. Besides an incomparable view and frontage on Briggs Marsh, the property included a single one-story barracks, one of seven barracks on the East Reservation site. Rather than tear it down, the Thornes followed a long-standing Little Compton tradition of repurposing and often moving old buildings.

The twelve-man barracks is now a one-story wing extending east from the main part of the house. Not large enough for their needs, the Thornes looked around for more surplus property. In March 1955 they purchased a two-story army "saltbox" from Harry Richmond's property for $1,500 to be "moved immediately." This structure had served as the base admin-istration building in the front yard of Richmond's Seaconnet House.

A neighbor remembers, at age eight, peering out his window to see a two-story saltbox rolling down the lane from West Main Road to the Thorne's new lot.[11] There the two structures were connected and placed on concrete piers. The Thornes acquired basic frame structures with open spaces and few fixtures. Army design included white clapboards and asphalt roofs outside, six-over-six double-hung windows, pine floors and five-panel doors inside. Partition walls were few.

In keeping with traditional Little Compton architecture, the new owners clad the house in white cedar shingles. The wing was divided into two bedrooms and two bathrooms. In the main house the Thornes eliminated central posts in the living room by spanning the ceiling with beams salvaged from an old mill. To enhance views over Briggs Marsh, they opened a twelve-foot wide section of the east wall and installed glass panels floor to ceiling. The expanded living room was made cozier with a new fireplace and brick chimney. A bump out addition was attached to the south, housing a kitchen.

In the saltbox portion the owners added a new front door surrounded by colonial revival trim, and laid a maple floor in the entrance room and a fancy oak floor in the den. Green painted shutters were hung all around.

The upstairs was divided into a maid's room and a "bunk room" for children over new oak flooring. A walk-in linen closet was added, plus two new bathrooms. Additional six-over-six windows facing east and west brought in more light. One visitor remembered a bank of army-vintage combination-lock mailboxes upstairs.

THE LUNT HOUSE

After thirteen years the Thornes, who were getting older, felt unable to take care of the house. In October 1967 they sold the property to Storer Boardman Lunt, known as "Bunty" to friends.[12] He was president of the publishing house W.W. Norton in New York City, but hailed from Portland, Maine. Finding such a peaceful spot not too far from the city was appealing both for vacations and as a place to retire. Soon Mr. Lunt could be seen rowing his skiff across the pond in jacket and bow tie for a neighborly lunch.

That same year in December he and Margaret K. McElderry, a fellow book publisher, were married in England. McElderry later became known as the grand dame of children's publishing. As a book editor, first at Harcourt Brace, then at Atheneum, McElderry helped turn children's literature into the profitable industry it is today. She actively sought out authors who were not afraid of controversial subjects and trusted her own taste. Although she would only publish books she loved, she was aware of their commercial potential. "It doesn't hurt to have a book that sells awfully well once in a while," she said.

In 1970, Storer Lunt retired and set about making a few alterations so the house would be more comfortable year-round. These included a new shed dormer, an extra bathroom and electric baseboard heat.

Otherwise not much changed on the inside. Storer bought the house with all the Thorne contents and furniture, as did the current owners. These included two antique Dutch Kas, one from Mrs. Thorne's grandmother. These locked cupboards were common in the seventeenth and early-eighteenth centuries. They held valuable linens, porcelain, silver and sometimes the household gun. Some were more than eight-feet tall. The second Thorne Kas was cut down as a low sideboard. Both pieces remain in the living room today.

Storer spent more time enhancing the space outside. Over the years he planted thousands of daffodils north and east of the house and new fruit and specimen trees. As a lover of birds, he let native species of bush and tree take over the margins of the property, now a complex haven for wildlife.

The Lunts had just ten years together. "Bunty" died in 1977. McElderry continued to edit books into her nineties. She died in 2011 at the age of ninety-eight after forty-four years sojourning at Briggs' Marsh. McElderry had no children. Her heirs included one of her famous authors — Susan Cooper. McElderry's estate sold the property to Bart and Elisabeth Brownell in January 2012.[13]

A NEW LEASE ON LIFE

The Brownells had fallen in love with the property, but so had raccoons wintering in the crawl space and mice nesting upstairs. After seventy years the house was in need of a serious restoration.

The challenge was to update for the twenty-first century without destroying history and charm. Renovations included lifting the house four feet in the air, digging a new foundation, strengthening framing, building a kitchen addition and installing new utilities. Thereafter the plan was to save as much of the old as possible.

The 1940s windows were restored. In the living room picture windows from the Thorne's time were replaced. A new entrance allowed the old den to double in size. In the wing, five-panel doors from army days were re-installed with rim locks and porcelain knobs. Sagging sheetrock was replaced with plaster and old floors carefully refinished. A new front door, rescued from a

Lunt House Renovations, 2013. Photo by Bart Brownell.

Taylor's Lane re-hab, was found in the barn of a local carpenter. In the master bedroom a new dormer opens up views to Martha's Vineyard.

In a final surprise, the Brownells discovered they were coming full circle to a salt pond across which their Southworth forbearers set up their first farm in the 1680s. After years of living abroad and moving house, the Brownells, their children and grandchildren had finally found a new and old home.

REFLECTING THE PAST

In the seventeenth century, the way land ownership was understood by the early English settlers and by the Sakonnets differed. And it differed too when the owners of land in the 1940s discovered that their land could be taken by the government if needed.

The manner in which the land was distributed to a select group of people in the 1600s and the 1900s is surprisingly similar. However, the intent behind those distributions differed dramatically. In the 1600s the Proprietors acquired and shared large tracts of land to encourage expansion and development. In the 1900s the land was purchased by a group of local residents to minimize expansion and development.

In the late 1800s, Sarah Orne Jewett described Little Compton as like "the places one goes on the way to sleep." Another said that "nothing ever happened" here.[14] As the world gets more crowded, this is the appeal of a town that encourages the creative reuse of historic buildings and the preservation of historic landscapes.

Works Cited

Arnold, James M. *Vital Records of Rhode Island 1636-1850.* Providence: Narragansett Historical Pub. Co., 1891.

Fall River News and The Taunton Gazette. *A descriptive and biographical history of Bristol County, Massachusetts.* The Boston History Company, 1899.

Findings for the Fort Church Military Reservation. Little Compton, RI: US Army Corps of Engineers, 2006.

Garner, John. *World War Two Temporary Military Buildings.* US Army Corps of Engineers, 1993.

Griehl, Manfred. *Luftwaffe Over America.* Mechanicsburg, PA: Stackpole, 2004.

Historic & Architectural Resources of Little Compton, Rhode Island. Providence: Rhode Island Historical Preservation Commission, 1990.

MacDonald, Ian. Interview. 2015.

N, F. *"Genealogical."* Boston Evening Transcript 24 Oct. 1906.

Reports of Cases Argued and Determined in the Supreme Court of Rhode Island [1849]. Providence: J.H. Bongartz, 1909.

Schroder, Walter K. *Defenses of Narragansett Bay in World War II.* Providence: Rhode Island Bicentennial Foundation, 1980.

Sherman, Robert M., and Ruth Ann Sherman. Vital Records of Marshfield, Massachusetts to the Year 1850. Providence: Society of Mayflower Descendants in the State of Rhode Island, 1970.

Shurtleff, Nathaniel Bradstreet. *Records of the Colony of New Plymouth, in New England.* Boston: Press of W. White, 1855.

Stratton, Eugene. *Plymouth Colony, Its History & People, 1620-1691.* Salt Lake City, UT: Ancestry Pub., 1986.

Taylor, Tom. Phone Interview. 5 Feb. 2015.

Textile World. November, 1921. New York, N.Y. : Bragdon, Lord and Nagle.

Wasch, Diane et al. *World War II and the U.S. Army Cantonment Construction.* Washington DC: United States Department of Defense, 1992

Wilbour, Benjamin F. *Little Compton Families,. Vol. I.* Little Compton, R.I.: Little Compton Historical Society, 1967.

Wilbour, Benjamin Franklin. *Notes on Little Compton from Records Collected by Benjamin Franklin Wilbour.* Little Compton, R.I.: Little Compton Historical Society, 1970.

2000

2012 *Bart & Elisabeth Brownell*

1967 *Storer Lunt & Margaret McElderry*

1954 *Norrish & Zoe Thorne*
1954 *Sakonnet Properties*

1942 *United States Army*

1926 *Ervin Dunn*

1917 *George Miller*

1900

1903 *Manuel & Rose D'Avila*

1894 *Frederick R. Brownell,*
Pardon C. Brownell & George Gray

1871 *Edward W. Howland*

1863 *John B. Howland*

1813 *Peleg & Sarah Bailey*

1803 *Isaac & Sarah Bailey*

1800

1777 *Captain John & Lydia Bailey*

1740 *John & Mary Bailey*

1712 *Lieutenant Thomas & Mary Bailey*

1700

1698 *John Bailey of Portsmouth*

1690 *Nathaniel & Phebe Warren*

1600

Bailey Farm – Summer Kitchen. *A woman washes dishes while Mrs. Bailey sits to the right.*
Painting by Sydney Burleigh. Courtesy of Janet Lofsky.

The Baileys of Bailey's Ledge

FROM FAMILY FARM TO SUMMER HOMES:
THE HUNTOON HOUSE •
THE STROBELL-GOODRICH COTTAGE

By Marjory O'Toole

While Thomas Bailey's descendants were building their lives on Warren's Point, his brother William Bailey's offspring were doing the same on Bailey's Ledge. The Huntoon House and the Strobell-Goodrich Cottage now sit on land that belonged to William's branch of the Bailey family and was once known as the James Irving Bailey Farm.

Patriarch John Bailey (1653-1736) of Middletown was the first to start to piece together this homestead farm eventually comprised of one fifty-acre lot and numerous eighteen-acre lots. All of the land was originally purchased from the Sakonnet Indians by Little Compton's First Proprietors in 1675. Nathaniel Warren acquired four of the eighteen-acre lots in 1690 and sold them to John Bailey in 1697. John bought three more from Joseph Church in 1710 for 250 £. John offered all seven lots, or approxi-

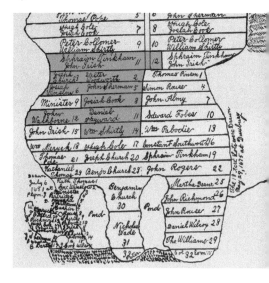

William Bailey's Lots. Detail of the Proprietor's Map. LCHS Collection.

mately 126 acres, to his son William who used the land to establish a family farm that provided comfortable and even prosperous livings for six generations of Baileys.[1] The exact acreage would change over time as lots were purchased from neighbors or inherited by descendants.

John never lived in Little Compton himself, but like many seventeenth-century American fathers, he purchased land for his sons and helped them establish their own households. Again like many of his contemporaries, and perhaps as a measure of paternal control, John did not formally give the property to his sons until his death, when he left the lots to them in his will. Son William passed away at the age of forty-six, six years before his father. William was the first of several Bailey patriarchs to pass at an early age leaving their widows and children to carry on without them. William's 1730 will divided his property between his four sons giving each boy very specific parcels of land, but it was not until his father John's will confirmed the bequests in 1736 that they became official. William's sons Captain Samuel Bailey and John the Second received the lots that eventually contained the Huntoon House and the Strobell-Goodrich Cottage.[2]

William (1684–1730) & Dorothy Graves Bailey (1684–1771)

William and his wife Dorothy had ten children between 1707 and 1727. All of the children's births were recorded in Little Compton, indicating that the couple was living on their Bailey's Ledge farm as early as 1707. Their daughter Lydia seems to have died young as she is not mentioned in her father's will. Like many Little Compton farm families the couple probably started housekeeping in one or two modest rooms and then expanded their home as their family grew and their pocketbook allowed. By all accounts William and Dorothy did very well during their twenty plus years of marriage. William was able to contribute a significant amount of acreage to the property by purchasing a fifty-acre lot (Number 11) from Thomas and Edward Gray in 1722.[3]

Another measure of their success was slave ownership. William and Dorothy were among the approximately twenty percent of Little Compton families who owned slaves at the time. William's will and the inventory of his personal property list a "Negro" woman named Millor who was valued at 30 £ and a "Negro Boy" named Guy who was valued at 60 £. Guy may have been Millor's son but there is no known evidence to support this. While the births of Little Compton's white children were very carefully recorded, the births of children of color were not.

Besides his land, Guy was William's most valuable possession. Guy's value was twice that of Millor's, a prediction of the value of work expected from a healthy young man over the course of his lifetime. As a possession, or human chattel, Guy was bequeathed in William's will to his son John the Second in 1730. In 1757 Guy appears again in John the Second's probate inventory, this time with a value of 350 £. At that time John willed Guy to his son Ephraim who was only thirteen. Ephraim's mother Elizabeth would have had responsibility for Guy until Ephraim came of age at twenty-one and was legally old enough to own property.

Ironically, the little "Negro Boy" with no birth record became one of the best documented African Americans in eighteenth-century Little Compton. Because Guy was passed down through three generations of Baileys, he appears in the Little Compton probate records far more often than most of the community's enslaved people. Legally, Guy would have had no say whatsoever in the way he was inherited. How- ever, even as a slave, Guy may have had some choices in life. He was baptized in the Congregational Church in 1742 and entered into full communion in that church in 1743. Guy Bailey also legally married Ann Pearce, the enslaved servant of James and Martha (Wilbor) Pearce, in 1750. It is possible that Guy was forced or strongly encouraged to make these choices, but only a very small number of Little

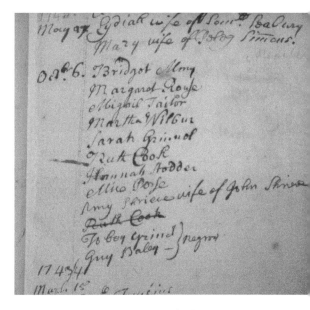

Congregation Church records showing Guy's baptism. LCHS Collection.

Compton's slaves appear in the church registers or marriage records. These were unusual choices for enslaved people, and it is very likely they were Guy's own choices. Of course they were made only with the permission of his owners. Since Ann was enslaved by a different family it is unlikely that the couple was able to live together. However, slaves typically had free time on Sundays, and they may have been able to see each other then. In 1755 James Pearce's probate records list two "Negro" boys, Jack and Abraham, who were probably Guy and Ann's sons.[4]

When William died, his widow Dorothy, age forty-six, was left with young William who was twenty-three and already a competent farmer, Sarah who was twenty and one year away from marrying, Priscilla who was eighteen, Samuel (17), Abigail (13), John (10), Elizabeth (8), George (5) and Ruth (3). Her father-in-law took steps in his will to make sure that Dorothy had an income from the farm until her children reached maturity, but once they were grown, there was nothing in either her father-in-law's or her husband's will to provide for her. Dorothy would be at the mercy of her children, but seemed to do quite well, living to the ripe old age of eighty-eight and leaving a comfortable personal estate to her daughters and granddaughters. Dorothy and William's dwelling house, barn, orchard and their land to the south went to their son Samuel. Several eighteen-acre lots to the north went to John the Second, and their son George received the fifty-acre lot at the far north edge of the property. Oldest son William received 500 £ instead of land, most likely to buy his own farm elsewhere.[6]

At that time boys were traditionally given land when their parents died. Girls were given personal or "moveable" property that they could take with them to their husbands' homes. Married women's possessions immediately became their husbands'. As a widow Dorothy had more rights than her married friends. She exercised one of them a year after her husband died by buying five more acres of land from Edward Gray adding to the land that would support her young family.[7]

Benjamin Franklin Wilbour writes in *Little Compton Families* that the original Bailey home was located in the orchard.[8] That original homestead was eventually torn down. Deacon George W. Church, who was born in 1816, recalls this happening "in his youth." The orchard still exists today, and is now the site of the Strobell-Goodrich Cottage. (See page 142 for that history.)

John Bailey The Second (1720–1757) &
Elizabeth Pabodie Bailey (1723–1802)

While his brother Samuel inherited his parent's home, John the Second built a house just a short distance away for himself and his wife Elizabeth whom he married in 1743. It is possible that their home is now the oldest portion of the Huntoon House. The home's main fireplace appears to be from the mid-eighteenth century. According to an old custom the fireplace builders hid items in the open space behind the brick to protect the home from evil spirts. These items, including silver shoe buckles, were found over 150 years later by the Huntoons.[10]

Sadly the superstition was not enough to protect John from an early death. Elizabeth and John had ten children before John passed at the age of thirty-seven in 1757. He wrote his will a month before his death leaving his sizable estate in Elizabeth's care until his children came of age.[11]

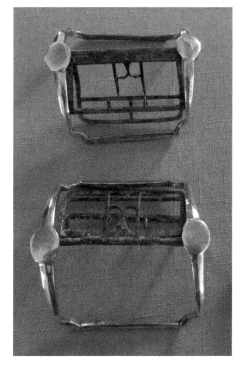

Eldest son Ephraim who was just thirteen when his father died was to receive the bulk of the land, over 100 acres and the family home, when he turned twenty-one. Ephraim was also to be the third and last master of Guy the family's "Negro" slave.

Ephraim's four brothers, two of whom were still babies, received much smaller lots along with sentimental items like their father's gun and silver tankard to help remember him. His four sisters were given money, between 100 and 130 pounds each with the older girls receiving slightly more than their younger sisters. John gave his "Negro" woman Peg to his wife Elizabeth. He also wrote that at Elizabeth's death Peg was to be shared by his two eldest daughters Elizabeth and Comfort.[12] Thirty-three years after

Silver shoe buckles found behind the Huntoon House fireplace. Courtesy of Janet Lofsky.

John's death, in the 1790 Federal Census, this branch of the Bailey family reported one enslaved person in the household. Most likely it was Guy who was listed in the records of the United Congregational Church as late as 1788. By the time of the 1800 census the family had no more slaves and in a few decades would become abolitionists.[13]

Elizabeth's family carried on for six years after her husband's death as a single-parent household, helped undoubtedly by the labor of Guy and Peg as well as the care and companionship of the many Bailey family members living nearby. Brother-in-law Captain Samuel Bailey and his wife Sarah Church lived right next door with their seven children. After twenty years of marriage Sarah Church passed away at the age of forty-two. Her youngest child was just two years old.

Now a widower with seven minor children Samuel sought the help of his sister-in-law Elizabeth. In just over a year the two were married in Tiverton, and their first child, Lydia, was born five months later. The seventeen Bailey cousins were now step-siblings, and Samuel and Elizabeth completed their family with son Benjamin two years later in 1766. Their marriage united not just cousins but large tracts of Bailey land, at least until Ephraim came of age and took possession of his inheritance. Together Samuel, Elizabeth and their children ran a large family farm that focused on producing woolen cloth from their flock of over thirty sheep as well as cider from the family orchard.[14] Samuel and Elizabeth also suffered the loss of four children – an all too common experience throughout eighteenth-century Little Compton and New England.

The presence of more than one house on the Bailey farm complicates the farm's history. Samuel inherited his parents' older home in the orchard, but who lived in what house, especially once Samuel married Elizabeth? Did the situation change when young Ephraim married? Samuel's probate documents shed some light on the subject. They describe a well-furnished home that contained a "great room," a sign that he and Elizabeth, with their younger children, were living in the old family house in the orchard. The great room had a bed standing in it and a large fireplace. The house also had a kitchen, a kitchen chamber or bedroom, as well as a northeast bedroom and a northwest bedroom and a garret or attic. It may have contained even more rooms, but they were not mentioned. Samuel seemed to have especially spoiled his sixteen-year-old daughter Hannah giving her a very fashionable dressing table and a side saddle.[15]

John and Elizabeth's newer home technically belonged to their son Ephraim after John's death. Ephraim would have been thirty-one, married and a father three times over when his Uncle Samuel died in 1775. Elizabeth was left a widow with minor children a second time. She buried Samuel with his first wife in the Old Burial Ground on the Commons, and when her time came in 1802, Elizabeth chose to be buried with her first husband John.

Ephraim Bailey (1744–1820) & Mary Briggs Bailey (1746–1819)

Unlike his father and uncle, Ephraim Bailey succeeded in living to the ripe old age of seventy-six. Mary, too, lived a long life dying one year before her husband at the age of seventy-two. During his lifetime Ephraim increased the size of the family farm by adding land that had once been his Uncle Samuel's as well as buying land from his own sons Ephraim and Peabody. He and Mary had nine children. Their youngest, Rebecca died at the age of twenty. At his death Ephraim gave his eldest son George a large lot of land, but following a common New England tradition, he gave his second son John the family home.[16]

John Bailey (1770–1860) & Thankful Cook Bailey (1782–1874)

John and Thankful Bailey surpassed all previous generations by living to age eighty-nine and ninety-one respectively. The Bailey's were prominent members of the United Congregational Church, and Thankful was one of twelve members who resigned from the Church in 1843 until it adopted an official position against slavery.[17] A local history written by Caroline Strobell, one of the Bailey orchard's twentieth-century residents, notes the presence of "Aunt Thankful's Well" on the property.[18]

The couple, who had a twelve-year age difference, married in 1801 and had just three children. Their eldest son George lived on the Commons operating a store with his wife and children. They later moved to Boston.

John and Thankful's youngest child and only daughter Ruth never married and like many single women of her time worked as a "tayloress."[19] She passed away one year after her father in 1861 at the age of fifty. She left her small estate to her nieces and nephews and forgave the money they had borrowed from her. James, the couple's middle child was slated to inherit the family farm.

James Bailey (1805–1849) & Abigail Coe Bailey (1810–1898)

Sadly another early death changed the family's plans, and James never owned more than four acres of the family land. At first James was not sure he wanted to be a farmer. As a young man he was a merchant like his brother George.[20] James married Abigail Coe in 1832 and their first child, James Irving was born the following year.[21] James and his young family were living in Westport, but fatherhood may have convinced him to return to the family homestead. In 1843 he bought four acres from his father that contained the farm's newer house for the very generous price of $125.[22] James became a full-time farmer working closely with his family members and holding the expectation that when the time came, he would inherit much more land from his father.

James, however, never inherited the family farm. He died in 1849, without a will, at the age of forty-three leaving Abigail a widow for the next forty-nine years. As a young woman Abigail Coe Bailey knew tremendous loss. Her second child Arthur Tappan died at the age of three. Her sixth child Abby Augustus died at nine months. She and her five remaining children mourned James's death together, and she was comforted by them as they grew. She and the children lived in their own home without live-in servants.[23] A map from 1850 shows Mrs. A. Bailey living in a cluster of Bailey family homes - next door to her in-laws John and Thankful Bailey and her husband's uncle Peabody. Her oldest, James Irving was just sixteen when his father died but had already been well trained in husbandry. He helped his grandfather John run the farm and continued to attend the local school.[24] In November of 1857 tragedy struck again, and two more of Abigail's children died, this time due to a

Mrs. A. Bailey's House. Detail 1850 Map of Little Compton. LCHS Collection.

pandemic influenza outbreak that circled the globe at that time. John Almy Bailey was nineteen years old, and his sister Sarah Amelia was eighteen. Now left with just three boys, James Irving, Edward and Erastus, Abigail continued to live among her Bailey in-laws who by all accounts were very good to her.

Despite the tragedies in her life Abigail was no shrinking violet. Caroline Strobell writes that Abigail "was a strong character and probably like many of her neighbors a believer in women's rights. In fact in those days there was a lively woman's suffrage movement up and down the road….Mrs. [Sydney] Burleigh can remember Abigail, in her white cap topping a false front, sitting in her favorite place…looking eagerly to see what was going down the road."[25] Abigail worked hard to provide for her family and help her son James Irving have what her husband could not have. Shortly after her husband's death Abigail invested her money with a group of relatives and neighbors and made a small profit.[26] In 1859 she purchased Peabody Bailey's fifty-six-acre farm from his heirs. Peabody and his family were already living part of the year in Providence. His widow Susan and his son Thomas chose to sell their riverfront Little Compton home for $3,450 and live in the city year round.[27] Fifteen years later, once her children were grown and her need for income less, Abigail sold the farm to James Irving for exactly the same price.[28]

In the meantime James Irving was doing his own purchasing. In the late 1860s James bought his brothers' shares of the family house and its four acre lot for $600 each. Both Edward and Erastus were living in Topeka, Kansas at the time.[29] James Irving also managed to do something his ancestors had been unable to do since their arrival in Little Compton. In 1870 he purchased "The Minister's" lot from the United Congregational Society.[30] The eighteen-acre lot was set aside for the town's minister in 1675 and was never developed. For almost 200 years it remained the property of the Church and jutted into the Bailey homestead breaking up the continuity of the farm. The Church may very well have allowed the Bailey's, who were members of the congregation, the use or rent of the land, but it was not really theirs until James Irving made his purchase.

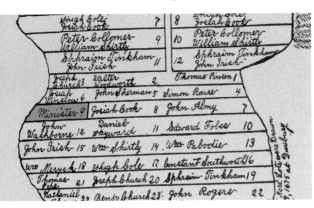

Detail of Proprietor's Map showing the Minister's lot. LCHS Collection.

When family patriarch John Bailey died, not only did he leave most of the family farm to his grandson James Irving, he also made provisions in his will to ensure the care of his daughter-in-law Abigail. John's widow Thankful received one third of the real estate. James Irving received the rest as long as he met two conditions. First, he was to allow his mother "improvement" or use of the property until March 1, 1863. (The significance of that date is unknown.) Second, James Irving was to pay his Uncle George $100, his Aunt Ruth $300, his brothers $100 each and his mother

$25 per year as long as she remained a widow.[31] Abigail never remarried and lived to eighty-seven. Presumably James Irving paid his mother $25 a year for thirty-eight years, a total of $950. John Bailey wrote his will in November 1857, the same month he lost his two beloved grandchildren to the influenza epidemic. He died three years later in 1860. He was eighty-nine years old.

Fourteen years later when Thankful Bailey died she also remembered Abigail with a gift of $25 in her will. Grandson James Irving received Thankful's third of the property and the "rest and residue."[32] With the help of his mother Abigail, James Irving Bailey had succeeded in piecing back together a farm that had been split into much smaller pieces by generations of inheritance. In fact the 135-acre "James Irving Bailey Farm" was just a little larger than the one his Great-great-great-great-grandfather John of Portsmouth created 200 years before.

Without land of their own James Irving's brothers needed to earn their livings another way. In 1860 at age eighteen Edward was working in Little Compton as a schoolteacher. A few years later he had packed up and headed West to make his fortune. Edward settled in Topeka, Kansas, married and raised a family. He never returned to Little Compton, though his children would eventually become the Bailey Farm heirs. Around the time of his twenty-first birthday Erastus joined Edward in Kansas but was back in Little Compton by 1875. According to Sarah Soule Wilbour's diary entry for October 4, 1890, "the most interesting neighborhood gossip just now, is the engagement of Erastus Bailey and Leonora daughter of Philip and Meribah Chase, he is a Deacon of the Church, she is a member."[33] Erastus married the fourteen-year younger Leonora Chace and ran his own farm on South of the Commons Road. Like many turn-of-the-last-century Little Compton couples, they had no children.

Erastus and Leonora Bailey. From the B.F. Wilbour Scrapbook. LCHS Collection.

The Baileys were indeed part of a neighborhood that included several other homeowners in this collection of house histories. Sarah Soule Wilbor socialized with and frequently wrote about them. Abigail Coe Bailey and Sarah Soule Wilbour were close friends. The James Irving Baileys, the Henry Richmonds and the Albert Seaburys were part of a vibrant circle that operated a Social Library, had tea parties, hosted clambakes, joined forces for charitable projects and sought each other's advice. Sarah noted many of these small but important events in her diary. From her we also learn that James Irving Bailey was called just "Irving" by his friends.[34]

Sarah Burleigh, the young bride of artist Sydney Burleigh also wrote about the Baileys. When Sarah arrived in Sakonnet for the first time in 1870 she remembers them living in one of the very few houses at Sakonnet Point. "The Bailey Farm belonged to Mrs. Abigail Bailey. She was quite feeble but very bright. Her son, James Bailey and his wife lived there with her. He was a fine farmer and kept everything there running nicely."[35]

James Irving Bailey (1833–1904) & Betsey Palmer Bailey (1840–1908)

When he was thirty-four years old James Irving married Betsey Palmer and took on his role as head of a household that in 1875 included his mother, his brother Erastus and a fourteen-year-old-servant girl from Newport named Lizzie Ryan.[36] James Irving and Betsey never had children, leaving the Bailey home childless for the first time in its history. James Irving's mother Abigail lived with them until her death in 1898. The makeup of the household changed throughout the years. Erastus moved into his own home. A cousin Deborah P. Bailey moved in to help with the housekeeping, and the number of servants and farmhands living with the family increased.

In 1880 Mary Bradley of New York, twenty-year-old Johan Schanz, and fifteen-year-old Joseph, who had no last name listed, from the Azores[37] provided the hard labor required to run the farm. Neither man could read nor write.[38] Twenty years later there were four Azoreans living in the household: Manuel Bernardo, Manuel Gomez, Antoine Machal and Rosa Sylvado, all young people in their twenties who had each been in the

United States for less than five year. None could read nor write. These young immigrants saved their money, encouraged their relatives to join them in Little Compton and helped form a new generation of residents who continued the local farming tradition throughout the twentieth century.

An 1870 map shows two homes on the James Irving Bailey Farm. James and Betsy's large house at the end of their drive and a smaller house near the orchard. The Benajah Borden Homestead was to the east. To the south, Deacon James H. Bailey was a cousin descended from Captain Samuel Bailey. His home became the Sakonnet Golf Clubhouse. James Irving's farm focused on dairying with a herd of thirty-two cows. There was also a large flock of poultry, most likely Rhode

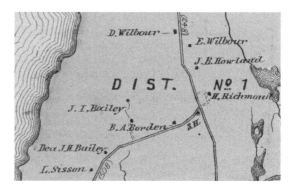

Map showing location of James Irving Bailey's farm. *1870 map. LCHS Collection.*

Island Red hens. Crops included apples, corn and other vegetables, as well as hay. A modern mowing machine helped with the haying.[39]

Caroline Strobell's history states, "James Irving Bailey became a famous farmer. Great stone out-houses bounded the home on the northeast, and on the northwest was the red carriage house where lived the help. Near this was a deep ice-house where were stored the apples and pears for which the farm was noted. There was also a huge barn which dominated the landscape….When James Irving and Betsey, his wife, developed the farm it became a land flowing with milk and honey. There was maple syrup from the trees, geese and Rhode Island Reds in the lanes, both famous in the New York market, cider ground in the one-horse mill, rows of cheeses in Betsey's cheese room, and butter on the hangshelf in the cellar. But the water in the kitchen well did not suit Cousin Debby Bailey, for she always took her pail down to her Aunt Thankful's well….Whenever you came into the house you would see the women spinning the distaffs in their belts and their hands going…as if they were playing the flute. When [Sydney Burleigh's father George] walked across the fields to the

James Irving Bailey. From the B.F. Wilbour Scrapbook. LCHS Collection.

Point, he used to stop on his way back and carry home a can of milk in on hand and a pat of butter in the other."[40]

James Irving did well during his lifetime due to his own labor as well as that of the women and servants in his household. Farming enabled the Baileys to accumulate numerous bank accounts and investments including five shares of the Seaconnet Steamboat Company.[41]

On a summer day the Seaconnet Steamboat Company brought as many as 300 visitors from Providence to Sakonnet Point, a well-established summer resort at that time. It is on one of those steamboats that the farm's future owners first came to Little Compton for a summer holiday and liked the area so much they decided to stay.

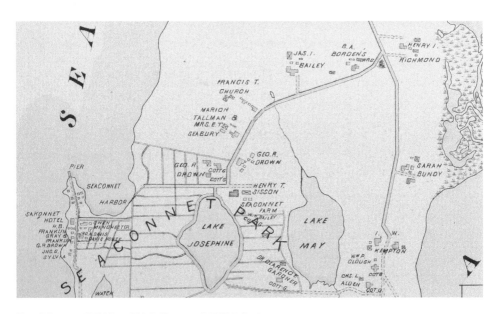

Detail from an 1895 Map of Little Compton. LCHS Collection.

James Irving Bailey died intestate in 1904. Family legend has it that he died in the act of trying to sign his will.[42] Without a will and because he had no children of his own, the farm was divided into shares and distributed to ten heirs including his wife Betsey, his brother Erastus, and his nieces and nephews from Topeka. None of the heirs was eager to continue the 200-year Bailey Family tradition of living and working on Bailey's Ledge. Erastus, the executor of his brother's estate, sold the 135-acre family homestead to Beatrice Sturgis Bartlett, the wife of Philip Bartlett of New York in 1907.[43]

SUMMER PEOPLE

Beatrice Bartlett was one of a number of New Yorkers looking to buy a summer home in Little Compton around the turn of the last century. Mrs. Bartlett did not keep the property long. Within five years she sold it to Henry Goodrich, another New Yorker with an interest not just in a summer home but in a development project.[44] He had the Bailey farm surveyed into lots, created the Compton Realty Corporation and began distributing land to investors and selling it, often to friends. A large portion of the farm became the back nine holes of the Sakonnet Golf Club. The James Irving Bailey House was sold to dear friends Harrison and Jeanette Huntoon, and The Orchard became the property of sister-in-law Caroline Lloyd Strobell.[45] The Goodrich, Huntoon, and Lloyd families have summered or lived year-round in Little Compton ever since and have made important and lasting places for themselves in the community.

Please see page 132 for the Huntoon House History.

Please see page 142 for the Strobell-Goodrich Cottage History.

The Huntoon House. Photo by Bart Brownell.

The Huntoon House

A GATHERING PLACE

By Marjory O'Toole based on an Interview with Janet Lofsky

Harrison & Jeanette Huntoon

Newspaper editor David Patten, a descendant of the Wilbour Family, introduced Harrison Huntoon to Little Compton. According to his son Howard Huntoon:

> *Before we moved down here in the summertime, about 1916, my father knew this David Patten who lived up West Main road opposite the Historical Society and he used to write for the [Providence] Journal. They would come down together on the boat – leave Providence in the morning and come down on the Islander and have a clambake at Lyman's Inn and then take the boat back in the afternoon, make a day's trip out of it. I think that's how my father first started coming to Little Compton.[46]*

Around the turn of the last century Harrison Huntoon was the successful owner of the Providence Braid Company and a widower. His two sons Harrison and Maxwell attended Moses Brown School. The motherless boys were taken under the wing of their pretty, young Latin teacher Jeanette Dickie Birdsall the daughter of a blind Quaker minister from Wallkill, New York. One day the boys asked their father to come by in a horse and buggy and purposely introduced him to Miss Birdsall. Soon there was a wedding.

Jeanette, who was called "Dickie" by the children, was twenty-two years younger than her husband and only eight years older than her step-son Harrison. The couple bought the James Irving Bailey House and the nine acres surrounding it from the Compton Realty Corporation in 1918 for the token amount of $100.[2] Jeanette and the children would

Harrison Huntoon & Jeanette Birdsall Huntoon.
Courtesy of Janet Lofsky.

Harrison, Jr. & Maxwell Huntoon.
Courtesy of Janet Lofsky.

Jeanne & Howard Huntoon.
Courtesy of Janet Lofsky.

spend the summer there, and the elder Harrison would join them on the weekends taking the steamship to Sakonnet Point or the train to Tiverton. The Huntoons added additional space and some early twentieth-century touches to the old house, including bay windows and up-to-date bathrooms, but the large eighteenth-century hearth still formed the heart of the home. Jeanette and Harrison also added children to their home, Jeanne and Howard were born just seventeen months apart. By all accounts, the Huntoons were an especially happy family. Young Harrison and Maxwell were devoted to their step-mother, and Jeanne and Howard were inseparable.

As children Howard and Jeanne would go behind the big fireplace in the dining room. One day they came out with two large silver shoe buckles, a silver bracelet and a small child's shoe. Hiding shoes in the space behind a fireplace was an old English custom to prevent evil spirits from entering a home. Based on the presence of the eighteenth-century shoe buckles as well as the mid-nineteenth-century child's shoe from Henry Daggart's "Fashionable Shoestore" in Boston, it is possible that two different generations placed "concealment shoes" behind their brand new fireplaces. John Bailey the Second and Elizabeth Bailey were the most likely builders of the oldest part of the Huntoon House. The couple was married in 1743 and would have hidden the objects in their brand-new home in the mid-1740s. James and Abigail Bailey were newlyweds

The Huntoon House. Pen and Ink by Patsy Compton. Courtesy of Janet Lofsky.

in the mid-1830s and were the most likely to hide the child's shoe behind a new parlor fireplace added to the back of the eighteenth-century kitchen hearth. Both couples hid the items for good luck and to keep themselves and their children safe. Sadly, both John and James Bailey experienced very early deaths leaving their widows to carry on. The Huntoon's story was similar.[3]

Harrison Senior was interested not just in enjoying his summer home but also in operating a gentleman's farm. He built a large barn that was only recently taken down and employed the Texeira

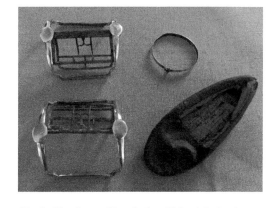

Shoe buckles, shoe, and bracelet found behind the fireplaces in the Huntoon house. Courtesy of Janet Lofsky.

The Huntoon Barn. Courtesy of Janet Lofsky.

family and later the Marion family to run the farm and keep an eye on things while the Huntoons were in Providence.

Harrison did not get to enjoy his farm for long. He died at age fifty-five leaving Jeanette a widow at only thirty-two. She never remarried. Harrison Junior took over the Providence Braid Company but he, too, died very young at thirty-two of pneumonia. It was now Howard's turn to run the family business. Running the company provided Howard with a good living but required him to put some of his personal ambitions aside. After graduating from Phillips Academy in Andover, Massachusetts he hoped to go to college but instead, at age eighteen, went right to work. Later he was eager to enlist in World War II, but the government would not allow him to do so. His factory was making parachute cord essential to the war effort, and he was required to stay stateside and manage the operation.

Joseph and Helen Marion

Jeanette raised the children in Providence in the winter and in Little Compton in the summer. In 1921 she almost doubled the size of the property by purchasing several lots from the adjacent Benajah Borden estate, one of which she later sold to the Sakonnet Golf Club.[4] On the farm Jeanette was helped incredibly by the presence of Joe and Helen

Marion. Over the years the Huntoons and the Marions formed a special bond. Joe Marion converted the upstairs of the new barn into a comfortable three-bedroom carriage house for his family that grew to include two children, Jean and Joseph Junior. According to her granddaughter Janet Lofsky, Jeanette was blessed to have the Marions. Joe was the farm manager and gardener as well as her driver, and Helen was the best cook and housekeeper in Sakonnet. They stayed on the property until Jeanette died, and then were invited by the family to stay as long as they wanted.

Janet says, "The Marions were my second parents. I could understand Portuguese, and Helen taught me to knit. We were always giggling. I remember sitting on the back stoop where we would shell peas, corn, and lima beans. Grandmother and Helen would be canning all throughout the summer. What we couldn't use ourselves, we shared with others. When we arrived for a visit my mother would sometimes have to remind me to go see Grandmother before I went to visit the Marions. I would play softball with young Joe and go collect periwinkles with him and steam them. The Marions were just a part of the family. It was a dream childhood."

Helen Marion in the garden. Courtesy of Janet Lofsky.

GRANDMOTHER'S HOUSE

Once her children were older, Jeanette Huntoon began to spend both summers and winters in Little Compton. Janet recalls that she was a "Fairy-Godmother-type person" who would draw people to her. "Everyone would visit Mrs. Huntoon when they would come to Little Compton. You just sort of checked in with her because you loved her. She was in a wheelchair for ten years – always dressed with her pearls – in a lot of pain but you never knew it."

Janet MacPherson Lofsky is the daughter of Jeanette's daughter Jeanne and Gordon MacPherson. Janet started her visits to "The Bailey Farm," as her family always called it, when she was just three weeks old in 1948. Her family would come down from Milton, Massachusetts. They stayed in the big house for the first few years and in 1953 built a small cottage of their own on a corner of the property on Bailey's Ledge. When Gordon MacPherson retired in 1960, he and Jeanne expanded their cottage into a larger year-round home. This home now belongs to Janet and her husband Norman.

The MacPhersons would come to Little Compton almost every weekend, year-round, and celebrated their holidays there as well. Janet laughingly remembers one Christmas when the family was placing the tree in her grandmother's bay window and discovered a bird had come in with it. In summers Janet spent her days running back and forth between her parents' cottage and her grandmother's house to watch Lowell Thomas and *To Tell the Truth* with her every evening.

Janet remembers that the house had seven bedrooms and five bathrooms. There were lots of nooks and crannies, perfect for hide and seek. The attic was a wonderful place with a wooden spiral staircase. It was filled with treasures and trunks for dress up. "Each morning Grandmother would be out in the garden whistling to the Bobwhites, picking her roses, and I would run out in my nightgown and bare feet to help her."

Jeanette Huntoon and Granddaughter Janet MacPherson Lofsky.
Courtesy of Janet Lofsky.

Jeanette continued to brave the Little Compton winters until her arthritis forced her to make a change. Each winter she would take a train to Tucson, Arizona. She would live in apartment in the city and go out to the Navajos to volunteer as a teacher. She would stay in Tucson January through March and return to Little Compton for the better weather. Jeanette enjoyed summers at the Bailey Farm for the rest of her life.

Howard & Sally Huntoon

When Jeanette passed away in 1968 her children Jeanne and Howard split the property. The siblings agreed that it was best if Howard, who was very handy, keep the historic home. Jeanne continued to enjoy her time on the Bailey Farm in her more modern house and also kept the barn with its carriage house as a summer home for Janet and her family.

Howard Huntoon in his Garden. LCHS Colllection.

The Bailey Farm continued to be the family gathering place. Howard and his wife Sally used the Bailey farmhouse as their summer home, and then in the late 1960s moved to Little Compton full time. Jeanne and Gordon also became year-round residents at that time and brother and sister were frequently in each other's homes. Step-brother Maxwell, who married into the Goodrich family, lived on Warren's Point Road, and he and his children all became part of one big extended family centered on and near Bailey's Ledge. Howard continued to be active in the Providence Braid Company until his death. The business is now in the care of the fourth generation of Huntoons.

The landscape surrounding the house was just as important to the extended Huntoon family as the house. A beautiful allée of Linden trees planted in 1887 by Betsey and James Irving Bailey leads from Sakonnet Point Road to the front of the home.[5] An enormous American Elm tree, one of the few to survive the disease that spread through the region, stands at the southeast corner of the house. It is well over one hundred years old. Howard enjoyed gardening on the property and was known to say that he lived a long life because he ate a head of lettuce every day.

Nancy Huntoon and Bill Forsyth's Wedding Party in "The Trap" in 1977. Courtesy of Janet Lofsky.

There is also a lovely sunken garden to the west of the house that is surrounded by stone walls and features an area with a garden bench that is affectionately called "The Trap." The spot has been the site of several weddings. Gordon MacPherson and Jeanne Huntoon were the first to be married there, and Gordon slyly gave the spot its name. Since then Nancy Huntoon and Bill Forsyth held their wedding reception there, and Janet MacPherson and Norman Lofsky were married in "The Trap." Though the property is usually called the "The Bailey Farm" or "The Huntoon House," many people also refer to it as the "Daffodil House" as the grounds erupt with thousands of yellow blooms each spring. The bulbs were planted many years ago by Jeanette Huntoon with the help of Joe and Helen Marion.

After Howard passed in 2005 the property was sold out of the family to new owners who are now carefully stewarding the historic house and creating their own family history there.

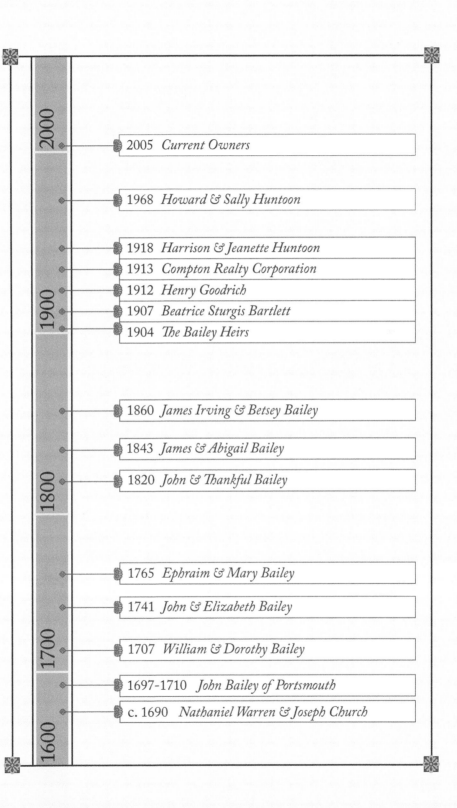

2000

2005 *Current Owners*

1968 *Howard & Sally Huntoon*

1918 *Harrison & Jeanette Huntoon*
1913 *Compton Realty Corporation*
1912 *Henry Goodrich*
1907 *Beatrice Sturgis Bartlett*
1904 *The Bailey Heirs*

1900

1860 *James Irving & Betsey Bailey*

1843 *James & Abigail Bailey*

1820 *John & Thankful Bailey*

1800

1765 *Ephraim & Mary Bailey*

1741 *John & Elizabeth Bailey*

1707 *William & Dorothy Bailey*

1700

1697-1710 *John Bailey of Portsmouth*

c. 1690 *Nathaniel Warren & Joseph Church*

1600

The Strobell–Goodrich Cottage. Photo by Bart Brownell.

The Strobell-Goodrich Cottage

TWENTIETH CENTURY LIFE IN THE ORCHARD

By Claudia Cooley Bell

This inviting cottage was built early in the twentieth century on land owned by Caroline Lloyd Strobell. Adjacent to the Sakonnet Golf Club, it sits in the midst of property that was once the orchard of the Old Bailey Farm and has been referred to as "The Orchard" ever since. Located on Bailey's Ledge Road, the property has been in the Goodrich/Lloyd family for the past century. Five generations have spent summers in this haven, enjoying the simple pleasures of a small New England town by the sea.

OWNERSHIP OF THE OLD BAILEY FARM ORCHARD

Henry Wickes Goodrich, a New York lawyer, spent many summers in Little Compton eventually buying a substantial house and barn on Sakonnet Point Road for his family. In 1912 Henry and his wife Madeleine Lloyd Goodrich purchased the nearby 135-acre James Irving Bailey Farm as an investment.[1] The following year that property was deeded to the Compton Realty Corporation that had been formed to hold and develop the land.[2] The Corporation's investors included Henry, his two brothers-in-law, and his wife's sister, Caroline Lloyd Strobell.[3] In 1916, Mrs. Strobell, known to her family and friends as Caro, used her shares to take possession of the section of the Bailey Farm known as "The Orchard."[4]

Soon after acquiring The Orchard, Caro built her modest cottage on the property where she resided from May through September for the next two decades. This wood-shingled structure has an end-gable-roof and an asymmetrical four-bay façade. The stone walls surrounding the property on the north, south, and east were also built about that time.[5]

THE PLACE I LOVE BEST

At the time she acquired The Orchard, Caroline "Caro" Lloyd Strobell was no stranger to Little Compton. She spent summers visiting her sister, Madeleine Lloyd Goodrich (wife of Henry W. Goodrich) and her brother Henry Demarest Lloyd. Her brother visited Little Compton for the first time in 1889 and a few years later, he bought thirty-two acres of property at the end of Sakonnet Point and built Watch House.[6]

Sisters Madeleine Lloyd Goodrich (L) and Caroline Lloyd Strobell (R).
Courtesy of Madeleine's granddaughter Frannie Huntoon Hall.

Like so many of her relatives, Caro developed a strong attachment to Little Compton. She was especially fond of her little corner of that world among the ancient trees of The Orchard. Living much of the year in the hustle and bustle of New York City, she found comfort in the natural beauty and quiet that surrounded her there. She came to The Orchard every summer, tending her garden and taking long walks. Her essay *My Apple Orchard*, written in 1939 (not long before she died) is a touching paean to this "place I love best."[7]

City-dwellers who have the good fortune of spending time in Little Compton can appreciate this excerpt from Caro's essay: "Coming to it [my orchard] from the city when spring is opening, being welcomed by the glow of daffodils, the blue clusters of grape hyacinths, and later the fragrance of apple blossoms – all under a wide arch of unsmoked sky – means entering a haven of peace behind which the troubles of the world seem to recede...." And then, with a touch of humor, she adds: "....unless the plumber has not come and you have lost your keys, etc., then world troubles are nothing."

The essay goes on to talk of the many old trees on the property and their historical roots. "This little acreage can indeed boast of an historical background, for as deep as the roots of my oldest Baldwins [an old variety of New England apple trees] so are the roots of the Bailey family in that same soil." Then, in recognition of the inevitability of loss, she laments: "...what with hurricanes and tempests, and the roiling of time, the Bailey orchard is writing its last chapter. Its regular rows are disappearing. One by one the old trees die and fall. On cool autumn evenings as I sit around my fire and watch their branches going up in smoke and flame, I think of the time when they were saplings, hopefully planted by young John and Thankful Bailey or their forebears, and of the time to come when like these founders, my orchard will only be a memory."

The property's current owner, Madeleine Goodrich Noble notes that her great Aunt Caro planted many trees that joined the original fruit trees. Among the oldest trees from the original Bailey plantings are a couple of mulberries that reportedly date back centuries.[8]

AN ACCOMPLISHED WOMAN OF STRONG OPINION

Born in 1859, Caroline "Caro" Lloyd was the daughter of Aaron Lloyd and Marie Christie Demarest Lloyd. After attending Vassar College, she taught school for a short time. Her first husband, Lothrop Withington from Massachusetts, was a genealogist with radical political views. They divorced, ostensibly after Caro learned that he had another wife in England. Lothrop later drowned in the sinking of the Lusitania in 1915. Caro's second husband, George Strobell, was a jeweler in Manhattan. Her grandnephew, David Goodrich, describes Caro as "always plainly dressed" and with "dark, almost fierce-looking eyes."[9] Grandniece Madeleine recalls that Caro was very hard of hearing and sometimes used an ear horn at the dining table.[10]

Caro was a writer, devoting a significant portion of her working life to compiling and editing the extensive papers of her brother Henry Demarest Lloyd following his death in 1903. After corresponding with dozens of his friends and associates, Caro composed a two-volume biography of her brother that was issued in 1912. Following completion of the biography, she organized her brother's correspondence and other papers and sent them to the University of Wisconsin in Madison for their archives.[11]

Documenting Henry's life was a daunting undertaking. A noted American journalist and social-economic reformer, Henry wrote and spoke extensively on a vast range of subjects, both in the U.S. and abroad. A champion of labor causes and a pioneer of the Progressive movement in the U.S., Henry Demarest Lloyd is best known for his 1881 *Atlantic Monthly* exposé of the methods used by John D. Rockefeller's Standard Oil to smother competition and his 1894 book *Wealth Against Commonwealth*. Some consider him to be the father of investigative journalism. In addition to his demanding career, Henry enjoyed a social circle that included people from all walks of life. Commenting on her brother's house in Little Compton, Caro wrote that "the front door was nine feet wide, typifying the house's breadth of hospitality."[12]

Caro admired her brother and his progressive philosophy, but her own political views were further to "the left." Writing articles for the Communist paper *The Daily Worker*, she eventually became one of its three female co-owners. Caro was comfortable with the unassuming Little Compton lifestyle. In contrast, she described nearby Newport as "marble palaces, homes reared on the proceeds of tyranny." Her grandnephew David Goodrich recalls that despite her radical political views, she was a popular member of the Little Compton Garden Club.[14]

WEATHERING THE STORMS

Lloyd Goodrich – Caro's nephew and one of Henry and Madeleine Goodrich's sons – came to The Orchard with his new wife Edith Havens not long after Caro built her house. In the summer of 1924, they lived in a tent on Caro's property. They were "roughing it" with a kerosene lamp for light and a nearby outhouse. One August night the couple was rudely awakened when a "nor'easter" blew down the tent, upended some furniture, smashed the lamp and ruined their books while also doing some damage to Caro's house. In a letter describing the incident, Edith noted that boats had been washed up on the shore in the harbor that stormy night and many fishermen had suffered serious losses.[15]

In 1930, Lloyd and Edith built more substantial accommodations in the northwest corner of Caro's Orchard – an unheated four-bedroom shingled house. It was not a fancy place – Phil Havens recalls that his Uncle Lloyd was adamant about constructing something "as economical as possible" – but as Lloyd's daughter Madeleine Noble notes, it did include exceptionally beautiful interior woodwork in vertical fir.[16] The two-and-a-half story shingled home has a center entrance framed by an arched trellis and tripartite windows. In 1938 Caro formally deeded the acre of land surrounding this house to her nephew Lloyd along with a right of way across her property.[17]

At some point (date uncertain) a third residence was erected in The Orchard – a very small one-story house that was built by Elisabeth Thomas, a close friend of Caro's niece and Lloyd's sister Constance Goodrich.[18] In 1940 Caro deeded the remaining share of The Orchard and its buildings to her sister Madeleine Lloyd Goodrich. This deed protected the right of Elisabeth Thomas to continue to reside in her little house on the property.[19] Soon thereafter, Madeleine – now a widow – moved

Hooked Rug depicting Miss Thomas' House.
A gift to the LCHS from her sister Margaret May Thomas.

from the original Goodrich house on Sakonnet Point Road to reside in the Strobell cottage next to her son Lloyd.

In a 1982 interview, Lloyd Goodrich talks about the special pleasure of residing in The Orchard: "It's a nice situation for us, like living in the middle of a park. There are only three houses on it. And we have an understanding with the Golf Club that no dwelling house would be built on the land which we conveyed to them."[20]

The Strobell Cottage, the Lloyd Goodrich House and Miss Thomas' little house have withstood many storms, including the disastrous 1938 hurricane that wreaked havoc on the Rhode Island coast. David Goodrich has vivid recollections of that momentous day watching the storm from his parents' house in The Orchard: "I was eight; Lloyd [father] was in Boston, giving a lecture. I stood by the window, staring, and apart from the fact that Edith [mother] cried out every time a tree came crashing down, I thought it was grand entertainment. The next day, I wasn't so sure: an *awful lot* of our trees were destroyed; there was sea water right up to our gate; there was this terrible story about five fishermen [who died]…people who walked to the shore found nightmarish rubble."[21]

THE OLD STONE WELL

One feature of The Orchard that has not survived is the old stone well that provided drinking water for the houses. The small illustration on the cover of Caro Strobell's *My Apple Orchard* depicts this well next to a tree. Recognizing the well's historic roots, Caro refers to it in her essay as "Aunt Thankful's well." Both Madeleine Noble (Lloyd and Edith's daughter) and her cousin Frannie Huntoon Hall remember the well and its clear, cold, delicious water. Frannie recalls that passing golfers would help themselves to a drink on occasion and that "the young, when height permitted, enjoyed hauling the wooden bucket up as high as it would go, then letting go of the rope and waiting for the splash below."[22] Madeleine notes that she was often delegated to pull up a bucket for drinking water at her parents' house.[23]

The demise of the old well was due to deliberate human intervention rather than the ravages of time or inclement weather. Lloyd Goodrich had it torn down and covered over in the early 1960s, fearing that his first grandchild might fall in. As Madeleine observes, "It had never worried

MY APPLE ORCHARD

By
Mrs. Caroline Strobell

Cover of My Apple Orchard an essay by Caroline Lloyd Strobell.
Courtesy of Frannie Huntoon Hall.

him when his own children or nieces and nephews were about, but such is the magic of grandchildren."[24]

THE HOLLYWOOD CONNECTION

Caro's radicalism generated many heated family discussions, but bonds within the family remained strong. One example is the close relationship she shared with her niece Frances Goodrich, daughter of Henry and Madeleine Goodrich and sister of Lloyd Goodrich. Lloyd's son David recalls that Frances "loved Caro dearly, but didn't buy her far-left convictions."[25] One subject they did agree on was the allure of summers in Little Compton. As a child, Frances spent summers with her family just down the road from the Bailey Farm. As an adult, she came to Little Compton

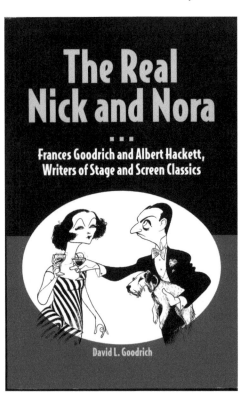

The Real Nick and Nora by David Goodrich.

with some regularity, visiting her Aunt Caro, her brother Lloyd, and her mother Madeleine at The Orchard, along with her sister Caroline (Tookey) Goodrich Huntoon and Tookey's husband Maxwell.

In collaboration with her partner and husband, Albert Hackett, Frances had a remarkably successful career as a dramatist and screenwriter. Together the couple produced thirty-three scripts that became major motion pictures. Many of these films, including *It's a Wonderful Life* and *The Thin Man* are treasured American classics. The lead characters in *The Thin Man* films, Nick and Nora Charles, are based to some extent on the Hacketts' own marital relationship and lifestyle. Frances' nephew David Goodrich captures the lives and times of this extraordinary couple in his memoir *The Real Nick and Nora* published in 2001 by Southern Illinois University Press. At the time the book was written, David Goodrich lived in his great Aunt Caro's cottage, and he composed part of the book while residing there.[26]

There is little doubt that Frances drew from her childhood summers in Little Compton in some of her writing. Moreover, Little Compton served as a welcome retreat for the Hacketts from the demands of their work and fast-paced social lives in New York and Hollywood. Following their first pressure-packed foray to Hollywood in 1931, they visited Frances' mother Madeleine, her sister Tookey and brother Lloyd, and her Aunt Caro in Little Compton. It was the perfect place to wind down, refresh the spirit, and reconnect with family. While there, Frances reported that, "Caro roamed the seaside links in the dawn hours alongside 'pompously parading seagulls,' memorizing a speech she'd been invited to give at her 50th Vassar reunion."[27] As a little girl in the 1950s, Janet MacPherson Lofsky, a Bailey's Ledge neighbor, remembers going with her grandmother Jeanette Huntoon to visit Frances Hackett in the Strobell-Goodrich cottage.[28]

THE AMERICAN ART WORLD CONNECTION

Lloyd Goodrich was a noted American art historian, promoting American art as an emerging genre and writing extensively on leading American artists of the time. Associated with the Whitney Museum in New York City for many years, Lloyd became its Director in 1958. In addition to his art history expertise, he was a strong advocate for improving conditions for the American artist. In his words: "The important thing is that we should recognize the value of the creative artist to our society and strive to reward him more adequately for what he contributes to our national life."[29] Phil Havens notes that both his Uncle Lloyd and Aunt Edith cared deeply about the civil rights of people and worked to protect them.[30]

Just east of Caro's house in The Orchard, there is a garage with a loft that Lloyd used as an office when in residence. Phil Havens recalls that as kids he and his cousin David were treated to quite an art education when visiting Lloyd in his study, viewing dozens of reproductions of art works of prominent American artists, including Eakins, Hopper, and Homer. Phil also recalls that another facet of his education was enhanced during visits to The Orchard....Elisabeth Thomas, the friend of the family who built and lived in the tiny house on the property, tutored him in reading.[31]

The garage housed Madeleine's Model A car. Although Madeleine owned the car, her daughter-in-law Edith was the one person on the premises who knew how to drive. "She chauffeured everyone around, to the library, to church, to Newport, where she said everyone spent their time looking back at Sakonnet."[32] On occasion, the garage became the site for making apple cider. Using a large, wooden press, cider would be squeezed from The Orchard's small apples along with some apples from the neighbors' trees. The product did not receive rave reviews. In Frannie Hall's opinion, "the Orchard cider was barely drinkable, but its manufacture was riveting to watch."[33]

PASTIMES AND HOUSEGUESTS

Swimming at the local Little Compton beaches was a favorite family activity. A 1932 painting by Molly Luce titled "Sand Dunes" shows Lloyd and Edith Goodrich with their son David, accompanied by Louise Havens and the artist herself enjoying a day at the beach. An alternative venue was the natural swimming pool on the south side of West Island, just a short boat ride from the mainland. Both David Goodrich and his cousin Phil Havens recall that their parents went there with friends in the 1930s and 1940s to swim and to picnic. "Sometimes, the picnickers stripped to go swimming; then, still nude, sipped drinks, ate lunch, and sketched and photographed each other."[34] Another painting by Molly Luce called "West Island" captures such a scene.

Houseguests are common for summer residents in such an idyllic seaside community. The Goodrich clan hosted their share, including a number of accomplished artists, poets and performers. One visitor in 1931, the Pulitzer Prize-winning poet John Gould Fletcher, expressed his thanks to Lloyd and Edith for their hospitality by writing: "I wish I were in your cottage....You do not know how good the days were...take a matchbox, fill it with Sakonnet sand, and send it to me post-post-haste....I want to remember that there was one place I enjoyed in America."[35] Another visitor was the American vaudeville and Broadway actress Beatrice Herford, known for her monologues lampooning popular figures. She

Sand Dunes. Painting by Molly Luce. LCHS Collection.

made quite an impression on young David Goodrich who recalls that "As a kid, I saw Beatrice perform several times in Caro's Little Compton living room: she was magical."[36]

RECENT HISTORY

Lloyd Goodrich became the sole owner of the two larger houses in The Orchard when his mother Madeleine passed away in 1949.[37] Following Lloyd's death in 1987, The Orchard property was co-owned by his two children, David L. Goodrich and Madeleine Goodrich Noble.[38] David inhabited their great Aunt Caro's cottage while Madeleine resided in their parents' house. David and his wife Patty made some interior renovations to Caro's cottage.

In a squib published in Chris Rawson's *Where Stonewalls Meet the Sea*, David jokes that he and Madeleine did have to cope with one consequence of living on property completely surrounded by the golf course – errant golf balls. While such balls have not broken any windows, "…enough wind up on our property that sometimes, walking around, we feel like farmers picking up eggs laid by free-range chickens."[39]

An author of fiction and nonfiction, David was based in New York but came up to Little Compton as often as possible. This history has drawn heavily on his two memoirs, *The Real Nick and Nora* and *My Well Spent Youth*. When David died in 2009, his share of The Orchard, including Caro's cottage, was left to his sister Madeleine. Living in Geneva, Switzerland for most of her adult life and raising her family there, Madeleine did not make yearly visits to The Orchard. Since her retirement, however, she has been spending her summers there, often in the company of her children and their offspring.

Today, the property known as The Orchard remains with a descendant of the Goodrich family who purchased it more than 100 years ago. While only a few of the old apple and pear trees are still standing, visitors to The Orchard will still sense its history and absorb the aura of tranquility and natural beauty that endures.

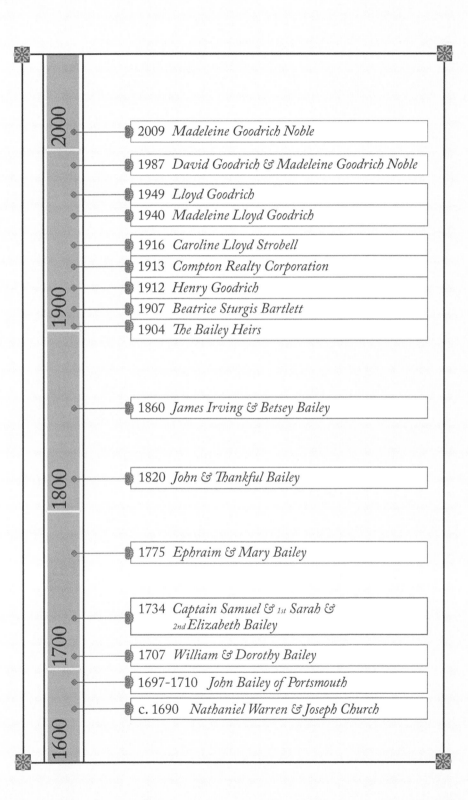

2000

2009 *Madeleine Goodrich Noble*

1987 *David Goodrich & Madeleine Goodrich Noble*

1949 *Lloyd Goodrich*

1940 *Madeleine Lloyd Goodrich*

1916 *Caroline Lloyd Strobell*

1913 *Compton Realty Corporation*

1912 *Henry Goodrich*

1907 *Beatrice Sturgis Bartlett*

1904 *The Bailey Heirs*

1900

1860 *James Irving & Betsey Bailey*

1820 *John & Thankful Bailey*

1800

1775 *Ephraim & Mary Bailey*

1734 *Captain Samuel & 1st Sarah &*
       2nd Elizabeth Bailey

1707 *William & Dorothy Bailey*

1700

1697-1710 *John Bailey of Portsmouth*

c. 1690 *Nathaniel Warren & Joseph Church*

1600

The Seabury House. Photo by Bart Brownell.

The Seabury House

A VICTORIAN GEM

By Marjory O'Toole

The Seabury House is one of Little Compton's very few Victorians. The farm's original colonial-era house was moved just to the north to make room for Albert Seabury's new house in the late 1880s. However, like all of Little Compton's farms its story began long before construction took place.

THREE-QUARTER-MILE-SQUARE

In May 1675, one month before the start of King Philip's War, Little Compton's English Proprietors wrote in their record book, "We bounded out unto Awashonks a parcel of land three quarters of one mile square joyning upon the south of the lotts first layd out to the proprietors."[1] Located just south of Taylor's lane, the Three-Quarter-Mile-Square was a parcel of land with rich soil. The Sakonnet River flowed by it on the west, and the Great West Road crossed through it on the east. It was very good land, but Awashonk's ownership did not last long.

There is no known record of the sale or removal of the Three-Quarter-Mile-Square from Awashonks, but by 1681 the Proprietors divided the parcel into thirty-two small lots and distributed them among themselves by lottery. At the time Awashonk's people most likely lived just to the east in the area now known as Wilbour Woods. Later they moved inland to the corner of East Main and Snell Roads. English settlers quickly began to establish farms on the Three-Quarter-Mile-Square lots. Several of those lots would one day be part of the Seabury Farm.

John Coe & Sarah Pabodie Coe

In the first few years of Little Compton's English settlement a very small number of men aggressively bought, sold and traded lots of land in order to establish substantial farms for themselves and their loved ones. Because of the various lotteries used to distribute land to the Proprietors a man might own isolated lots of land in various parts of town ranging in size from one hundred acres to ten. He and his neighbors would negotiate with each other to acquire adjoining lots and create farms large enough to support a family.

The Albert T. Seabury Farm contained land that, like five other properties in this book, was once owned by Nathaniel Warren. Because the land was not near his homestead farm on Warren's Point, Nathaniel was happy to sell the thirty acres (the southern half of the 3rd eleven-acre lot and the 16th fifty-acre lot) to John Coe in 1693, helping him build a family farm that started eight years earlier with a gift from his father-in-law.[2]

John's father-in-law William Pabodie helped John and Sarah establish themselves in Little Compton with a gift of two ten-acre lots from the Three-Quarter-Mile-Square. William Pabodie played an important role in the creation of the town, purchasing land from the Sakonnets and serving as an early town clerk. His wife Elizabeth Alden Pabodie is believed to be the first English girl born in New England.[3] Pabodie acquired many of

The Lots Owned by John & Sarah Coe. Three-Quarters-of-a-Mile-Square included 32 ten-or eleven-acres-lots.

the Three-Quarter-Mile-Square lots and established his own farm on the site. In 1685 he wrote, "For the love and good will and affection which I bear to my loving daughter Sarah and her husband John Coe of Boston... I do give three small parcels of land — two ten acre lots lying in the three quarter mile square" and one eighteen-acre lot (Number 27) in the Common Field. William had purchased Lot Number 1 from Joseph Church, and Lot Number 2 and Lot Number 27 from John Rouse of Marshfield. Lot Number 27 passed through several more hands including Nathaniel Warren and John Bailey.[4] Pabodie helped Coe again in 1694 by selling him the western end of the 17th fifty-acre lot for 30 £.[5] With three separate deeds and portions of five different lots, John Coe was able to piece together a seventy-acre family farm that supported his and other families for generations. His neighbors immediately to the north were the Samuel Wilbors.

The number and complexity of land transfers during the town's first few years is astonishing. Some were recorded with deeds registered in Plymouth or Bristol Counties. Others were simply noted in The Proprietor's Book that is today kept in the town vault. The stakes were high for these early settlers. A well-situated farm meant stability and financial success. Having family on neighboring farms meant plenty of hands to share the work. Because of William Pabodie's land deals both his son William and his daughter Sarah would live just a short walk away from his own home.

John and Sarah Coe had nine children. Their first two daughters were born in Duxbury, Massachusetts and did not survive. Once settled in Little Compton the family was blessed with seven healthy children. The names of their deceased children, Lydia and Sarah, were given again to their third and fourth daughters. When John died in 1728 his wife Sarah received all of his property to use for the remainder of her life. When she passed in 1740 at the age of eighty-six their eldest and youngest sons, Samuel and Joseph, split the seventy acres and the houses their parents owned at the time. Certainly the two brothers had already been living and working on the family property for many years. Their parents' deaths made their ownership official. Middle son John was given land in Maine, but ended up living on Taylor's Lane in Little Compton instead. His home was also on a lot that was once part of the Three-Quarter-Mile-Square.[6]

Joseph Coe (1700–1780)

Joseph, a bachelor, inherited the part of the farm that would one day become the Seabury Farm. His brother Samuel died just six months after their mother. Samuel's wife Mary paid his end-of-life expenses from his estate: the Reverend Richard Billings 14 £ for medicines, William Stevens of Newport 4½ £ for gravestones and Captain David Hilliard of Little Compton 1¼ £ to make the coffin.

When Joseph died thirty-nine years later in 1780 his will read simply, "I give and bequeath to my well respected nephew Benjamin Coe all my estate real and personal."[7]

Captain Benjamin Coe (1753–1818) & Sarah Simmons (1759–1823)

In the midst of the American Revolution Benjamin and his wife Sarah were married (1780) and lived in a one-and-a-half-story house on the property he inherited from his uncle Joseph. The house still survives today, relocated a short distance to the north. Either Benjamin or his uncle Joseph could have been responsible for the construction of the home. In 1781 the twenty-eight year old Benjamin was elected a Captain in the war effort (most likely of the local militia), and his home was used as one of Little Compton's five blockhouses during the war. Blockhouses were private homes manned by soldiers to keep a watch on the Sakonnet River. They were situated all along the Great West Road (West Main Road.)[8] The English enemy had seized Newport, and the threat of attack was very real for Little Compton's citizens.

Like many of their neighbors the couple had a large family of ten children between 1780 and 1800, and also like many families lost a child at a young age. When their fourth son Ezra came of age he settled just to the south of his parents at the corner of Swamp Road and farmed the adjacent land. He married twice, both times to a daughter of his neighbor Isaac Bailey.[9] Ezra's four brothers chose different paths. Each of them left town moving to Swansea, Newport, Block Island and even Virginia.

When Benjamin died in 1818 his wishes seemed simple enough. Sarah was to have life-long residency in the house, his unmarried daughters were

The Coe Blockhouse. Photo by Bart Brownell.

to have a room with a fireplace, and once Sarah died the property was to be divided among his five sons.[10] That wish set off a complicated series of land transfers, even a lawsuit, that ultimately resulted in Ezra Coe owning the entire property.

Ezra Coe (1787–1851) & First Sarah Bailey (1786–1817) & Second Deborah Bailey Bartlett (1780–1853)

Immediately after his father's death Ezra started to acquire his brothers' shares. Benjamin was a cordwainer or rope maker in Newport and quickly sold his share for $17.[11] In a less friendly exchange, Ezra sued his brother Joseph in 1821 because of a dispute over their father's estate. The Sheriff seized Joseph's share of the farm and Ezra was the high bidder at $25 when it went up for public auction.[12] Brother Samuel mortgaged his share to his Aunt Hannah Coe for $120 to help fund his adventures in Virginia.

Samuel defaulted on the mortgage, and Hannah sold the share for $150 to Ezra in 1836. Finally, in 1844 Ezra purchased the fifth from his brother Adam for a hefty $300.[13]

Ezra was eager to get that final fifth and was willing to pay a premium for it. He had a buyer waiting in the wings and a new business venture to fund. Just three weeks after purchasing Adam's share, Ezra sold the Coe family farm to James P. Sisson of Providence.[14] Ezra used the $3,500 he received to help his son Joseph create Little Compton's first grand hotel, the Seaconnet House. (Please see page 78 for a history of the Seaconnet House.)

James P. Sisson (1815–1861) & Mary Tew (1815–1885)

James Sisson, was one of the thirteen children of Lemuel Sisson, a tenant farmer from Newport who brought his Methodist religion to Little Compton. In the 1830s and 40s James' brothers were purchasing large tracks of land in the Sakonnet area, and he followed suit. Farming since childhood, James knew how to improve his land. In 1859 he purchased seaweed gathering privileges and a right of way from Michael Mosher to ensure his fields were well fertilized.[15] James, however, had more than farming on his mind. Encouraged by his brother David's business successes, James moved his family to East Greenwich by 1860 and pursued his own manufacturing career. Upon his death in 1861, James' family opted to stay in the city. They signed a deed to the town of Little Compton providing land for the Number 1 Schoolhouse and sold their farm to Benjamin Seabury, a man who made his fortune in another booming American business, seafaring.[16]

Captain Benjamin Seabury (1803–1892) & Elizabeth Tompkins (1807–1893)

When Benjamin was twelve years old he went to sea. By the age of twenty-three he was the master of his own vessel and by thirty-five retired from his seafaring life. He and his wife Elizabeth settled on South of the Commons Road and Benjamin built a store on the Commons that he operated for nearly forty years.[17] By all accounts he was a financially successful man. He bought the Sissons' West Main Road farm in May 1864 as an investment for the future.

Albert T. Seabury (1843-1922) &
Susan Burlingame (1841-1924)

That future had everything to do with Benjamin and Elizabeth's third son Albert T. Seabury. Unlike several of his brothers who left Little Compton to pursue business careers, Albert maintained his ties to the land and stayed in Little Compton. Albert married Susan Burlingame in December 1864, and the couple began to make a home for themselves on the West Main Road farm

The Albert T. Seabury House c.1910. LCHS Collection.

Captain Benjamin had purchased just months before. Albert added to the farm with his own purchase of fifteen acres of nearby pastureland in 1866.[18] The farm was a busy place. In 1879 Albert leased a small portion of the

property to Oliver Brownell to run a wheelwright shop, carriage manufactory and carpenter shop.[19] An insert from an 1895 map shows the location of the buildings.

Though they occupied it for a time, the mideighteenth century house that the Coes and the

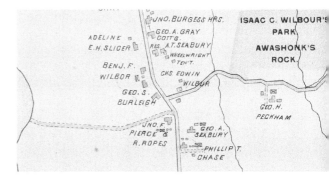

The Albert T. Seabury Farm in 1895. Map detail. LCHS Collection.

Sissons enjoyed did not suit this Victorian-era couple. Sometime after 1870 Albert and Susan had the house moved about an eighth of a mile to the north and built a home of their own. Today the old house sits just south of the New Wilbor Cemetery. The Seabury's new home embraced

Clambake at the Seabury House, c. 1890. LCHS Collection.

the style of the time as well as its more modern comforts. According to the 1990 architectural survey of Little Compton homes completed by the Rhode Island Historical Preservation Commission, the design appears to be inspired by the many house pattern books available in the nineteenth century.[20] The Commission dates the house to around 1880. In 1887

Albert officially bought the property from his father for "$1 and other valuable considerations."[21] This official purchase may be connected to the construction of the house.

Albert and Susan had two children who died very young, but the couple refused to be lonely. Their spacious new home became a social center filled with family and friends. They also forged strong relationships with younger members of their extended family and the people who helped

Albert & Susan Seabury.
From the Bejamin Franklin Wilbor
Scrapbook. LCHS Collection.

them run their farm. When Albert passed away in 1922 his will made arrangements for a $1,000 bonus to be paid to Cornelia Manchester as a reward for her continued loyal service to his wife Susan. In his last years Albert Seabury's life was an interesting mix of old and new. He invested in telephone and electric companies and owned an automobile, but he still had a variety of horse-drawn vehicles and still earned his income in part through his flock of ninety hens.[22]

Susan had life tenancy on the property but lived only fifteen months after the loss of her husband. Albert divided his belongings between two young male relatives both of whom shared his name. Albert Edwin Seabury of East Providence, who was perhaps a nephew, received personal property that included valuable investments. Albert Seabury Crandon, a native of Acushnet, Massachusetts, was named Executor and received the house and farm, furniture, farming implements, vehicles and livestock. Albert Crandon's connection to the Seaburys is obvious in his name, but it has been difficult to unravel the details of his relationship to them.

Albert Seabury Crandon (1893–1988) & First Grace Scully & Second Matilda Crandon

Albert Crandon was a young civil engineer working in the Pittsburg steel industry in the 1920s when he inherited the Seabury Farm. His wife Grace's family was from Pittsburg, and the Crandons and their two children lived there until they moved to Hartford, Connecticut around 1940. Because of Albert's work they could not live in Little Compton year round, but the farm became their summer home for over sixty years.

Albert settled the Seaburys' estates and found a farm manager he could trust to look after the property while he was away. Immediately following

Albert Seabury's death, Albert Crandon arranged for Joseph Lemar to live on and manage the farm. Lemar (now more commonly spelled Lima) was a forty-three year old Azorean immigrant. He and his thirty-year-old wife Delphina Star Lemar and their children lived in a cottage on the property, farmed the land and maintained the property so that all was well when the Crandons arrived each summer.

The Lemars and the Crandons signed a series of leases from 1923 through 1935 that formalized their arrangement. The Crandons kept the main house, its yard, a small storage shed, the south half of the cook house and the south half of the first floor of the shop for themselves. The Lemars paid $300 a year to rent the fifty-two acre farm and had the use of the cottage and all the other buildings on the property including the barn, the large hen house and the corn crib. The Lemars also had access to the orchard and a large garden. The lease actually required them to cultivate the garden and to share the fruits of their labors with the Crandons. The Lemars were also required to be good stewards of the land — rotating their crops, and using seaweed and all the manure the farm produced to fertilize the fields.

The Crandons called their Little Compton home "Old Elm" and through the years they became important and well-liked members of the Little Compton Community. Most residents today are too young to remember the Seaburys and simply call the property the "Crandons' House." Albert and his second wife Matilda eventually retired to Little Compton and became year-round residents. Matilda joined the Sogkonate Garden Club. Like most married couples they kept a few secrets from each other. Matilda was concerned for Albert's health and wanted to keep his ice cream consumption to a minimum. Albert outsmarted her by hanging a spoon from a string in the basement so he could sneak downstairs and eat ice cream right out of the freezer. In the 1980s they

Matchbook from Old Elm. Courtesy of Doug and Bonnie Brout. LCHS Collection.

Albert and Matilda Crandon. Courtesy of Doug and Bonnie Brout. LCHS Collection.

hired a local teenager to help them around the house. He remembers Mr. Crandon as "a very diligent and neat record keeper. He had a daily log and would enter my hours in his log by hand using a pencil." He also remembers their kindness. "When I graduated from eighth grade, Mrs. Crandon bought me a boom box. They were nice. I remember they allowed me to use their old Cadillac and take it to the prom."[23]

The Bradleys

Albert Crandon passed away in 1988. In 2007 his heirs sold the property to Carlton and Lisa Bradley of Hawaii. They enjoyed the farm as a summer home and frequently had tenants keep an eye on the property when they were away. During her term of ownership, Lisa Bradley both renovated and preserved the historic legacy and character of the property. Major improvements and modernization of the main house's systems, kitchen and bathrooms were completed with the utmost care and sensitivity to the property.

The Brouts

The current owners Doug and Bonnie Brout bought the house in 2013. As a result of their stewardship of the property, the historic house remains very unchanged from its original Victorian design but now provides a comfortable twenty-first-century country home for the Brouts and their two sons. The home's original fireplace made of beach stone remains the focal point of the living room. As they explored the property, the Brouts discovered that the barn and other outbuildings were filled with historical significance, too, and have vowed to uphold the integrity of all the buildings on the property. Like previous owners, the Brouts plan to continue to honor and enjoy the history of the house's role as a gathering place for family and friends. The couple is now working on plans for the farm's impressive stone barn to function as a family gathering spot, preserving this important structure as well as the nearby corn crib.

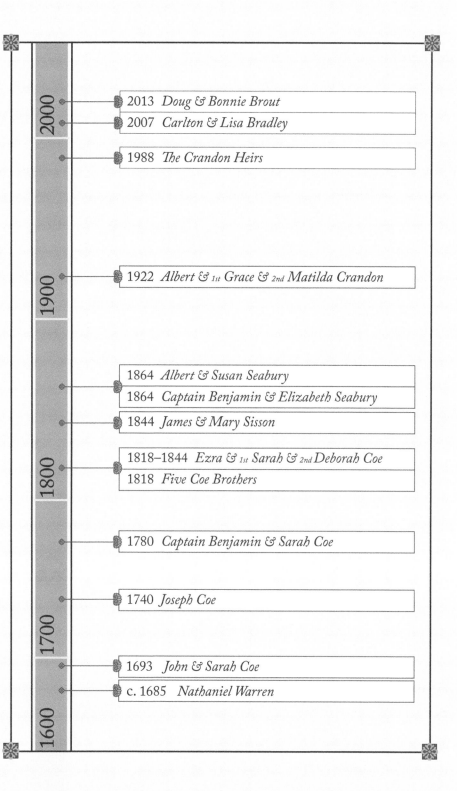

2013 *Doug & Bonnie Brout*

2007 *Carlton & Lisa Bradley*

1988 *The Crandon Heirs*

1922 *Albert &* 1st *Grace &* 2nd *Matilda Crandon*

1864 *Albert & Susan Seabury*

1864 *Captain Benjamin & Elizabeth Seabury*

1844 *James & Mary Sisson*

1818–1844 *Ezra &* 1st *Sarah &* 2nd *Deborah Coe*

1818 *Five Coe Brothers*

1780 *Captain Benjamin & Sarah Coe*

1740 *Joseph Coe*

1693 *John & Sarah Coe*

c. 1685 *Nathaniel Warren*

2000

1900

1800

1700

1600

The Head House. Photo by Bart Brownell.

The Head House

THREE HUNDRED YEARS AT GOOSEWING FARM

By Marjory O'Toole

THE SAKONNETS

Goosewing Farm lies midway between land once occupied by Awashonks and her people at Sakonnet Point and that of her step-son Mamanuah and his people at Acoaxet. Perched between Tunipus and Quicksand Ponds, the farm has provided fruitful hunting, fishing and farming lands for centuries.

THE FIRST PROPRIETORS

The farm was purchased by Little Compton's First Proprietors from Mamanuah in 1678 as part of a much larger tract of land. The Proprietors were comprised of a group of Plymouth colonists who were entitled by King Charles II to own land in the new world. They worked in concert to purchase Sakonnet and Acoaxet territories from the Sakonnets. The Proprietors divided the large tract of land encompassing Goosewing Farm into twenty-three thirty-acre lots and held a lottery in April 1678 to divide the land between twenty-five men (in two cases two men shared one lot).

The core of Goosewing Farm has always been the land known originally as Lot 8 and Lot 9. Over time the farm has increased and decreased in acreage as nearby lots were purchased or sold by

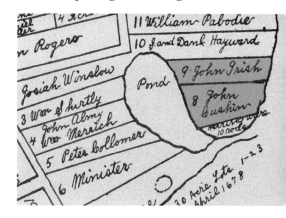

Goosewing Farm. *Detail of Proprietor's Map. LCHS Collection.*

various owners. Today the farm encompasses Lots 8 and 9 along with Lot 10 and a portion of Lot 2.

As a result of the Proprietors' lottery, Lot 8 was awarded to John Cushin and Lot 9 to John Irish. John Cushin (a.k.a. Cushing) of Scituate sold Lot 8 to William Pabodie of Little Compton in 1687. Like almost two-thirds of the Proprietors, Cushin never settled in Little Compton, but instead sold or traded his land to other Proprietors or young farmers from Aquidneck Island interested in land of their own. At some point Lot 8 passed from William Pabodie to Benjamin Woodward (aka Woodworth). Woodward then traded the lot to Henry Head Senior in 1692 in exchange for a different lot of land and eighteen pounds in silver money.

Head purchased Lot 9 directly from John Irish in 1708 for seventy-two pounds in silver money. John Irish figures prominently into Little Compton's early history. He was born in Duxbury in 1641 and as a teenager worked for Miles Standish. He moved to Little Compton after King Philip's War (1675-76) and established a large estate on West Main Road across from the Friends Meeting House.

THE HEAD FAMILY

As a result of these purchases and trades, Henry Head Senior united Lots 8 and 9 in 1708 creating the farm almost as we know it today. Head was born in England in 1647. In 1677 he was one of several skilled tradesmen invited by the First Proprietors to move to Little Compton and practice their trades for the benefit of the town. The Company of Proprietors offered Head a free ten-acre house lot in the Maple Avenue area and welcomed the surveyor, Free Mason and farmer into the community. The Company also invited Head to become a Proprietor himself by sharing in the expenses of all future land purchases from the Sakonnet Indians.

The said Company at hand granted unto Henry Head one house lot at Saconet provided he build and settle on the same within two years next after the tenth of May last past and pay the apportion of the purchase of ye said lands from the indians and other charges in & about the same, but if the said Henry Head Shall neglect to settle at aforeseaid then the said grant to be utterly void and the land to be & remain the full proprietors.[1]

Henry Head married Elizabeth Ketchum about 1677, and their oldest son Jonathan was born in 1678. Because of Head's two-year deadline in which to establish his household, Jonathan was likely born in Little Compton and may be one of the first English children born in town. Despite the family's modest start on just ten acres, Henry Head proved to be an astute businessman. Over the course of his lifetime he accumulated hundreds of acres in both Little Compton and Westport. (Though in Head's time it was all Little Compton.) In the final years of the seventeenth century he purchased large tracts of seaside land from Mamanuah and Mamanuah's sons William and John that included much of Acoaxet Neck.[2] Smaller purchases and trades with fellow Englishmen resulted in 140 acres on Maple Avenue surrounding his original ten-acre lot as well as substantial holdings between Adamsville and Quicksand Pond. His final purchase appears to be Goosewing Farm's Lot 9 from John Irish.

Head's purchases from the Sakonnets were not always made with the blessing of his fellow Proprietors. Both Head and Proprietor Daniel Wilcox found themselves in trouble with the rest of the Company for making unsanctioned purchases. Those purchases were seized by the Company, and Head and Wilcox were brought to trial in 1693.[3] Henry Head managed to make amends and continued to live peacefully in Little Compton for the rest of his life. Wilcox fled out of the colony to escape his punishment.

Shortly after his sanctioned purchase of Lot 9 in 1708 Henry Head Senior, who was now sixty-one years old, wrote his will bequeathing Lots 8 and 9, a total of sixty acres, to his second-born son Henry Junior. Head Senior passed away nine years later in 1716 leaving his children generous inheritances that included his own farm on Maple Avenue, Goosewing Farm, silver, bills of credit, bonds, thirty-two head of cattle and four slaves.[4]

The wording of Henry Senior's will makes it clear that Henry Junior was already living on Goosewing Farm in 1708. He and his wife, Elizabeth Palmer, welcomed their first child in 1709 and their tenth in 1727. Henry and Elizabeth's home was the first permanent dwelling on Goosewing Farm and most likely stood for just over 100 years, sheltering four generations of the Head family. Henry Junior was a carpenter and a surveyor as well as a farmer. His livestock included cattle, horses and swine. At his death he owned two oxen, nine cows, three horses, one pig, three geese and a turkey. Elizabeth and her daughters contributed to the family income by spinning and weaving and making cheese. Like his father, Henry Junior was a slave owner. He was the master of a "Negro" woman named "Frank" who in 1755 was valued at 0 £. Frank's lack of monetary value indicates that she was an elderly woman who had served the family for many years. Now in her old age the Heads were required to provide for her.[5]

The Heads' home included a "great room" that contained one bed in addition to a large fireplace used for heat and cooking, a "bedroom" with one bed, and a second floor "chamber" with one bed. There may have been other rooms not mentioned in Henry's 1755 probate inventory. His belongings included the "chest that I keep all my wrightins in" and two books, indicating a strong level of literacy.

When Henry Head Junior died on March 4, 1755 at the age of seventy-five he left Elizabeth:

my well beloved wife one room in said house that she shall see cause to chuse to be for her for her natural life and the choice of any one of my beds - and one third income from the estate – judged by unconcerned persons – 1/3 personal estate after debts paid hers forever[6]

Elizabeth does indeed seem to be a well-beloved wife, as Henry was especially generous to her in his will. Many Little Compton husbands left their wives property, income or personal belongings only as long as the wives remained their widows. If they remarried their inheritances would revert to their husbands' other heirs. Elizabeth was given her inheritance "forever."

Third son Benjamin received all of Henry's real estate including his homestead farm. He gave each of his other children 1 £ indicating that he had given them valuable gifts of property or personal belongings earlier. Henry seemed most concerned about his married daughter Elizabeth Jameson who was ill at the time. He left 40 £ in his will to pay for her "doctoring."

Henry was buried on Goosewing Farm. His beautifully carved gravestone cost his estate 23 £.[7] It was discovered over 200 years after his death upside down at the bottom of a fire pit. After spending many years at the Little Compton Historical Society the stone has recently been returned to its original location on the farm.

Benjamin Head Senior was born on the Head Farm in 1718 and lived there with his own family until his death in 1796. He married Judith Wait of Portsmouth in 1743, and together they had eight children. Benjamin replaced his father's old orchard with a "young orchard" and raised livestock that included cattle, sheep, turkeys and chickens listed as "Dunghill Fouls." He referred to different parts of the farm as "meadowland, pastureland and soft meadow."[8] Soft meadow likely referred to the farm's extensive salt marsh meadows.

Graveston from an abandoned grave-yard on a farm in Little Compton

Henry Head Junior Headstone. Sketched by Meredith Wildes in eighth grade, c. 1956.

Judith and her daughters were prolific spinners and weavers working with both linen and wool. Upon Judith's death in 1802 she left "33 skeins of linen yarn, 16 skeins of tow yarn, three skeins of woolen yarn" and a house filled with valuable linens including thirty-three sheets. Judith's probate inventory contains a detailed list of her garments providing us with a rare look at the type and quantity of clothing an eighteenth-century Little Compton woman would own.

> *One Dammas Gown, Two Calico Dittoes, One mueen, One velvet Cloak, One Bunnitt, Two pair of Shoes, Three Woollen Gouns, Six woolen Peticoats, Three woolen wescoats, Four linen collers, Three Woollen aprons, Three checked aprons, Six handkerchiefs, Eight caps, One pair of silver shoe buckles, Eight shirts, Six pair of Woolen Stockings, Two pair of mittts, Two pair of linen stockings[9]*

During his lifetime and through his will Benjamin Head Senior sold or gave four of his sons – Benjamin Junior, Henry, Lovett, and Gamaliel – pieces of the homestead farm. As a result three different houses stood on the property at that time. Henry, who was a weaver, purchased a dwelling house and an acre and a half of Lot 9 from his father in 1786.[10] He received another five acres adjacent to Tunipus Pond in his father's will. Benjamin Junior purchased a house and five acres from his father in 1794 and later inherited the heart of the homestead farm including land that stretched from Tunipus to Quicksand Pond.[11] Gamaliel owned a house and at least fifteen acres of land adjacent to Quicksand Pond. Gamaliel's property appears to be at the north end of the property. Lovett owned fifteen acres of land stretching between the two ponds that seems to have been sandwiched between Benjamin Junior's and Gamaliel's properties. Lovett, Benjamin and Gamaliel shared their father's salt meadows. Benjamin's fifth son John was given $100 at his father's death in 1796.[12]

Dividing the large farm into smaller pieces made it difficult for the Head brothers to make a living there, prompting them to seek other occupations or to move elsewhere. Lovett was a mariner living in Westport and sold his fifteen acres to Joseph Wilbor the Second.[13] Benjamin Junior lost five acres of the farm in 1786 to the "Keeper of the Grand Committees Office" to pay a debt, most likely taxes.[14]

Eight years later Benjamin Junior was forty-six years old when he married Hannah Grinnell just two years before his father's death. Very little is known about these Heads who do not appear to have any children recorded in Little Compton or any recorded gravestones. It is likely that they moved out of town after selling the property to Jonathan Peckham in 1812.

Because of the Head family's one hundred years at Goosewing Farm the nearby beach and creek became known as Head's Creek and Head's

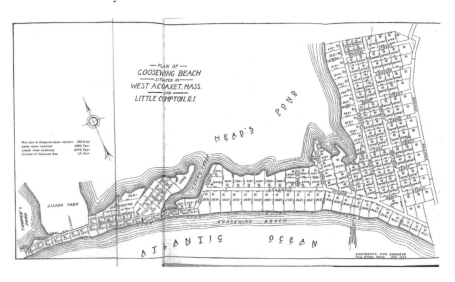

Goosewing Beach, 1925 Development Plan. LCHS Collection.

Women at Work in the Head House. Painting by Meredith Wildes Cornell. LCHS Collection.

Beach and appeared by those names on old maps. Even Quicksand Pond was known by some as Head's Pond. That name appeared in the twentieth century on a map produced by the Truesdale family.

THE PECKHAM FAMILY

Jonathan Peckham purchased forty-eight acres of farmland from Benjamin Head Junior for $4,000. The 1812 deed continues to refer to the land as Lots 8 and 9 and established the property's small cemetery as the Head family burying place forever. Recent architectural analysis of the property's historic Cape-Cod-style house completed by Lombard Pozzi dates the house to within a five-year period between 1810 and 1815. Based on the Peckham's purchase date, it is likely that they built this house. At the time, the original Head dwelling house would have been over 100 years old. Materials from the original house may have been recycled to create the Peckham's new home. The property's current owners, the Acebes family, completed extensive restorations of this historic building in 2008. That work was dedicated to the memory of the farm's original house and homesteaders, and as a result the home was named "Head House."

The Peckhams may also have been responsible for the "concealment shoes" found in a space behind the fireplace during the Head House's restoration. Hiding worn shoes near the openings of homes is an interesting European custom that found its way to seventeenth, eighteenth and even nineteenth-century America. The shoes were meant to protect the inhabitants from any evil that could enter the home's openings, namely windows, doors and chimneys. Worn shoes were often used not just for thrift but because they were more deeply connected to the users than new shoes and would therefore be more protective. Women's and children's shoes were most commonly hidden because of their close ties to the home. At Goosewing Farm restorations revealed a single child's shoe and a single woman's shoe hidden in an opening behind the downstairs fire box. The shoes are now on display in the Head House.

Though Jonathan and his family were the ones living on what was still known by the community as "The Head Farm" the property was clearly under the control of Jonathan's father Isaac. Upon Isaac's death in 1821 his will declared, "I also desire that my Head Farm, so called, be sold for paying of note to Sanford Almy, Isaac Wilbor, Joshua Austin, Thomas White, William White and Ephraim Gifford." The will gave Jonathan five dollars. Jonathan appears to have left town after he sold the farm to Peleg Brownell of Westport in 1822 for $4,500. The farm had grown to eighty-five acres by that time.

THE BROWNELL FAMILY

Eight years later in 1830, Peleg and Martha Brownell (and their son and daughter-in-law Peleg Junior and Desire) sold seventy-five acres of uplands, marsh and beach to Ebenezer Terry of Dartmouth for $2,500, a dramatic reduction in value even considering the ten-acre decrease in size. The deed listed eight acres of meadows, the "Herring weare" and the family burial ground as exceptions to the purchase. The herring weir was a small piece of public property at the southern tip of the farm that enabled all Little Compton residents to fish for herring.

THE TERRY FAMILY

Ebenezer and his wife Betsy quickly resold seventy-eight acres in 1833 in two deeds to Michael Mosher of Dartmouth at a combined price of $3,400 along with Mosher's promise to "support" all the line wall and fences along the property lines.

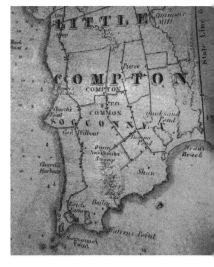

Detail from 1831 map of Little Compton. LCHS Collection.

THE MOSHER FAMILY

Twenty years passed before Michael Mosher sold fifty-nine acres to Levi W. Sisson in 1853 for $3,600. The deed included the rights to seaweed and "muck" on the beach. It is unclear where Michael and his family moved after Goosewing, but he continued to sell seaweed privileges to other farmers in the community who did not have access to beaches. James P. Sisson bought privileges from Michael in 1859 and used the seaweed as fertilizer for his farm on West Main Road.[15] Michael's wife Levina passed away in 1847 and was buried on the Commons. They had five children.

THE SISSON FAMILY

Levi W. Sisson was the son of Lemuel Sisson, the family patriarch who brought Methodism to Little Compton in 1816. After working as a tenant farmer, Lemuel quickly came to own the family's first large seaside farm in Little Compton, Seaconnet Farm at Sakonnet Point.[16] Levi W. was the eighth of Lemuel's thirteen children. From 1838 until his purchase of Goosewing Farm

Detail from 1850 map of Little Compton. LCHS Collection.

Levi W. Sisson and Mary Taber. Courtesy of Avis Buxton Child.

in 1853, Levi W. and his wife Mary Taber leased and ran his father's farm. Levi W. was known as a quiet man who suffered from recurrent bouts of ill health.

Levi W. and Mary had six children; four of whom remained unmarried and lived together in the now expanded Head House. Over time the Little Compton community began to associate the farm with the Sissons, and the term "Head Farm" was gradually replaced by "The Levi Sisson Farm" or later "The Sisson Farm."

Upon his death in 1880 Levi W. left the farm to his two youngest children, Lemuel and Levi. Levi continued to live in the Head House with his sisters and his mother until their respective deaths.

Sister – Elizabeth in 1885
Mother – Mary in 1889
Sister – Mary in 1902
Levi in 1908
Sister – Rachel in 1921

Detail from 1870 map of Little Compton.
LCHS Collection.

Detail from 1895 map of Little Compton.
LCHS Collection.

At the age of forty-five Lemuel chose to take a bride in 1894 and built a new, much larger farmhouse on the property for himself and his new wife, Laura Peckham. Laura was fifteen years his junior and was the daughter of Albert and Charlotte Peckham, the founders of Peckham's Greenhouses. The construction date of the house is confirmed by the builder's signature and date written on the stairs:

The Sisson Farm, c. 1900. The Head House is in the center. The Sisson House is to the right. LCHS Collection.

Built by Wm D. Gross
Sept. 5th 1894
of New Bedford, Mass.

The signature was hidden on the back of a stair riser but came into view during the Acebes' renovation in 1989 and is now preserved for guests to the Sisson House to see.

Lemuel Sisson. Courtesy of his granddaughter Avis Buxton Child.

Levi and Lemuel were engaged in general farming, stock and poultry raising. An early twentieth-century biography of prominent Rhode Island men lists Levi as a "quiet, genial, home-loving man, and while not a strong man physically he has always been a hard worker." He died at the age of fifty-six. Lemuel is described in the same biography as having a "quiet and industrious disposition" and as being "highly respected in the community." He, like many of his family members, was very active in the Methodist Church. Lemuel passed away in 1924, but his family remained on the farm for

The Sisson Family, 1902.
Standing from left to right: Laura, Lemuel, Flora Lewis –
a Servant, Rachel. Seated: Alice (born in 1902), Albert, Sidney,
Levi, William. Seated on ground: Unidentified woman holding
Sarah Lewis, Unidentified woman, Mary.

over twenty years more. Each of his children was given an equal share in the property. His youngest son Tom continued to work the land like his father and grandfather before him until his own death in 1944.

Lemuel's granddaughter Avis May Buxton Child remembers her childhood visits to Goosewing Farm in the late 1930s and early 40s and gives us some insight into the Sisson family and daily life on the busy Little Compton farm.

VISITS TO GRANDMOTHER'S HOUSE

Avis, her brother and her parents, Alice Sisson and Charles Buxton, lived in Charlestown, Rhode Island. Little Compton was "quite a trip" but the family made it on a regular basis to visit Alice's mother Laura Sisson and Alice's siblings on the family farm. When the Sissons knew that Avis and her family were coming, they would leave a lamp in the kitchen window. Avis could see the lamp as they approached the gate "all the way down the lane, and that was nice."

The Lane to Goosewing Farm. Courtesy of the Acebes Family.

One summer they stayed the whole summer because Avis' parents were not well. Otherwise it was a short visit, most often with just her mother but sometimes with her father, too. They would take the Saunderstown ferry to Jamestown and then the ferry to Newport. The alternative was to drive through Providence.

Avis remembers her grandmother Laura was always in a long skirt with petticoats, black stockings and black shoes. Laura and her adult children were very plain people and were very active in the Methodist Church. Laura was also very frugal. She had boxes and boxes of black stockings in the attic waiting to be repaired. The attic provided Avis with other information about her relatives. She never knew her grandfather Lemuel, but she did know that he grew turnips because of the seeds he left behind in the attic.

Uncle Tom Sisson ran the farm which was primarily a dairy at that point. Trucks would come frequently to pick up the milk, wholesale. The farm also produced hay. The barn was electrified even though the house was not, and there was a windmill to pump water. Avis' brother spent much more time in the barn than she did, though she does remember the barn cats well. One hired man worked with Uncle Tom, and though he did not live on the farm he took his noontime meal with the family.

Avis' Aunt Ida never married. "She lived with Grandmother and worked at the library with Mrs. Nancy Almy. Aunt Ida had a car and during World War II she would volunteer to spot planes, not on Goosewing – closer to Sakonnet," recalls Avis. "Aunt Ida had a radio in her room that was powered by a small windmill on top of the garage that brought electricity to a battery in her bedroom." That was the only electricity in the house.

The Sisson Farm Windmill.
Courtesy of Avis Buxton Child.

In the late 1930s and early 40s the Sissons lived much like they had in the nineteenth century. The farmhouse had no central heat. A stove in the kitchen burned coal briquettes, and there was a "collar" stove in the sitting room. At night family members would take bricks wrapped in paper bags to bed in order to keep warm. They used kerosene lamps and heated water on the stove for their baths. There was no indoor plumbing. The nickname for their three-hole outhouse was the "Kitty House." There was also no icebox. Avis remembers a "cool room" off the dining room that was used to store food. However, like many Little Compton families, the Sissons did embrace the telephone and had a phone in their home in the very early 1900s. A postcard of their gate shows the phone line running up the drive on thin juniper poles.

Meals were always served in the dining room. Avis' grandmother would ring the dinner bell and served jonnycakes three times per day. Fish from the surrounding ponds and beach were often on the menu. A big garden provided fresh vegetables with lots leftover for canning. Avis remembers Mr. Simmons delivering the groceries after the order was called in and Mr. Mulligan delivering the meat.

While Avis and her relatives lived in the 1894 Sisson House, the older Cape-Cod-style Head House was just across the yard. It was much expanded by this time and was rented out in the summer. Avis remembers the Hutchinson family summering there. Mrs. Hutchinson was there all the time. Mr. Hutchinson would commute back and forth from Fall River and their grown children would come to visit them.

As a young girl Avis would help with chores around the house which included preparing food, helping with dishes, emptying slop pails and trimming the lamps. She would also help take the family's clothes to the "Wet Wash," bring them back wet to the farm and hang them up on the line to dry. Each day marked a specific task – washing on Mondays, ironing on Tuesdays and so on through the week. Avis also remembers one summer when she and her brother saved all their money from picking and selling blackberries to buy tickets to a Red Sox game. Aunt Ida helped them by taking the berries to the library to sell.

Despite their chores there was plenty of time on the farm for fun. Avis and her brother would catch crabs in the pond and bring them home to eat, swim in the ocean – always with an adult looking over them, rummage through the old dump, visit relatives on nearby farms, play in the barn and the hayloft and gather around 7 p.m. to watch the New York boat go by. There were not many boats, and that was a highlight. Some days were spent with Aunt Ida at the library. Nighttime meant card playing and conversations, and Sundays meant Sunday School at the Methodist Church founded by Avis' ancestors.[17]

Goosewing Farm. Painting by Sydney Burleigh. LCHS Collection.

The Sisson family opened the farm's laneway to beach visitors in the 1930s as a way to supplement their income. They also rented space in the second lot up from the beach to families who camped for the summer.

CAMPING AT GOOSEWING FARM

Present day Little Compton resident Don Truchon lived in Pawtucket as a boy and fondly remembers camping at Goosewing Farm. His mother Janet (the ultimate good sport) spent entire summers, at first in a tent and later in a homemade trailer, with her two sons while Don's father Roy came on Wednesday evenings and the weekends. On Wednesdays young Don would collect a bushel of crabs, and on Thursday mornings Roy would take them to work at the Corning Glassworks in Central Falls to share with his friends.

Tom Sisson gave the Truchons permission to camp in the second field up from the beach along with several other families including Harold and Alice Lawrence, the Archer family and the Woods from Woods Bakery in Fall River. Harold Lawrence was a fight promoter, and Henry Archer was a policeman in Fall River. There was a fresh-water well for the campers' use and an outhouse at their disposal. Don remembers his father bringing drinking water in five-gallon glass jars protected by wooden crates with springs in the corners.

Sunbathing cows. Courtesy of the Moore Family.

Don also remembers being fascinated by the everyday operations of the farm. He would watch Tom Sisson's hired man Irving move the bull around with a long pole that hooked into the ring in the bull's nose. Don would also sit on the stone wall "helping" neighboring farmers Joe and Manny Rocha watch the cows that they would occasionally drive onto the meadows closest to the beach.

The greatest attraction, however, was the beach. Don says:

Most of my days were spent right on the beach or in the salt water for hours or with my mother and the other ladies at camp. Joe Couto was the lifeguard when the beach was run by Tom Sisson. Joe spent a great deal of time teaching all the kids in the compound how to swim. It became a natural thing because we were in the water all day.

Harold Lawrence would take his boat, which was on a trailer, move it onto the beach, roll out into the surf, and go to Cutty Wow and, in an hour maybe an hour and a half, he would be back with over a hundred pounds of fish. Harold would take his catch and go to Fall River to sell it in the fish market. He also had a crab pot, and he used to keep green crabs in there as bait for the tautog. It was always a threat to me whenever I misbehaved, which was several times a day as I remember it, my mother said I was headed for the crab pot. When I misbehaved in Pawtucket

she said I was on my way to Sockanosset, which was the bad boys' school.
But in the summertime it was out to the crab pot. I was never able to
figure out which was more fearful, Sockanosset or the crab pot!

World War II factors
strongly into Don's memories
of summers on the beach.
During the war all the campers
had to be outfitted with
blackout curtains, and Janet
Truchon would make fresh-
brewed coffee and pastry
for the soldiers walking the
beach on night patrol. The
camp's children incorporated
the war into their play and, in

Don Truchon, eight years old, piloting Harold Lawrence's boat to
catch eels in Tunipus Pond, c. 1943. Courtesy of Don Truchon.

their own way, understood the seriousness of the situation.

A stone wall gateway had a rock configuration that was very similar to
photos of the cockpit of a B-17 or B-24. That was my cockpit seat all
during World War II as a bomber pilot, and the other side of the entrance
to the lot was a much smaller and insignificant in my opinion rock
formation, and that was Ronny Tougas' seat. Half of the privy was
a toolshed, and in that toolshed Harold Lawrence had a hand-operated
grinding machine used for sharpening tools, knives, axes, whatever.
When cranked, it made a whirring sound very similar to a high-speed
engine. When I wanted my engines warmed up for my B-17, I had
Ronny crank that baby up, and you could hear it over in Westport.

We also had two rocks on the beach, my ship and Ronny's ship.
I would sit on that rock for hours and hours letting the tide come in.
I was looking for German submarines, which was very important!

The 1944 Hurricane blew the Truchons' camper away. The Woods'
camper was positioned pointing into the wind and survived. Losing the
camper was bad enough, but Don remembers one item that was a real loss.

My father had just purchased a pair of Florsheim shoes and those shoes were quite expensive. I remember spending from dawn until evening hunting for those shoes in the lot we camped in. Never found them. I think my father gave up on Florsheim and used a cheaper shoe from there on.

The family didn't give up on camping. They began using a 16' x 16' tent on a homemade wooden platform.

I remember vividly that every night my mother would be quite meticulous about setting all of the ropes that were there to stabilize the tent. It was crucial if you were going to have heavy winds.[18]

Once the Truesdales began to manage the beach, Dr. Truesdale employed Don at a rate of twenty-five cents per hour to sell soda, candy and ice cream from a shed in the parking lot. There was no electricity so the ice cream was packed in dry ice. Don supplemented his income by helping himself to the treats.

In 1937 parking on Goosewing Beach meant parking right on the beach.
Courtesy of the Philippi Family.

THE TRUESDALE FAMILY

By the 1930s Dr. Philemon Truesdale owned Goosewing Beach, but not yet Goosewing Farm. In 1944 and 1945 the five Sisson siblings each sold their share of the farm to the Truesdale family. The Truesdales continued to welcome visitors to the beach and ensured the farm was used for agriculture. Elizabeth (Libby) Truesdale Philippi was the beach manager from the early 1950s until her death in 1973. She and her husband Alexander were the owners of the Marsh House on Warren's Point.[19] They would rent the Marsh House each summer and move to the Sisson House on Goosewing Farm with their five children.

Libby was responsible for hiring the lifeguards and ensuring they were properly trained. A college-aged Don Truchon was one of the lifeguards who worked for "Ma Philippi" as he called her. The lifeguard sheds were on skids. Libby would call Chet Wilkie when a big storm was coming to pull the sheds a safe distance from the beach. There was a very popular shack on the beach that sold hot dogs and hamburgers, soda and other snacks. Libby would recruit her children for clean-up duty every Monday for fifty cents per hour. According to Libby's eldest daughter Elizabeth (Bunny) Millikin, it was hard work, especially cleaning out the "honey buckets" from the bathhouses. Bunny remembers a large billboard at the Long Highway gate to Goosewing Farm advertising, "Seaside Parking on Grassy Meadows." Hilda Wildes, the wife of Goosewing Farm's tenant farmer, was responsible for collecting money. Bunny says, "It was a wonderful place for people to come and enjoy the beach and the marsh. Mother really loved people and knew how to get along with them."

The much smaller town beach, South Shore, was adjacent to Goose-wing Beach on the west. Bunny remembers that each year the town would use heavy equipment to push the creek that separated the beaches a few feet to the east, thus gaining a little more room for the town beach by taking it from Goosewing Beach. Libby was aware that this was going on but didn't complain very much. She explained to her children that the town beach needed the space. Today

Libby Truesdale Philippi and her lifeguard son Eric in a Goosewing Beach boat. Courtesy of the Philippi Family.

Goosewing Beach is part of the Goosewing Nature Preserve and is owned and operated by The Nature Conservancy. Parking is at the adjacent town-owned South Shore Beach.

During the 1950s Harvey McArthur established a summer day-camp on Goosewing Farm. The camp used the farm's corn crib as its office, the large stone barn as an activity center and a nearby pit for archery practice.[20] In the late 1950s the Philippi family began staying at Marsh House for the summer, and the Truesdales rented the Sisson House to a number of summer visitors including Brent and Fay Moore and their children from 1971 to 1989. It was the Moore children Avila and Brent who found Henry Head's buried tombstone while they were digging up a shark's head they had buried the year before.[21] As a result of decades of beach parking, summer rentals and summer camps many local people have fond memories of Goosewing Farm.

The Truesdales cared for and improved the farm as well as the beach. In the mid-1940s the farm's nineteenth-century stone barn roof was in need of repair, perhaps as a result of the 1944 Hurricane. Tom Marvell, a young graduate from the Harvard School of Architecture and Dr. Truesdale's son-in-law, was given the job of redesigning it. They chose a gambrel style instead of the original peaked-roof because it increased the barn's ability to store hay by thirty percent. The Truesdales also ensured that there were tenant farm families living and working on the farm.

THE BIXBY FAMILY

Local resident Richard (Dick) Bixby remembers living at Goosewing Farm in the Head House as a fourth grader in 1945. His father Raymond was one of the men hired by Frank Hathaway to rebuild the barn roof. During the job, Raymond met Dr. Truesdale and was soon hired by the doctor to manage not only Goosewing Farm, but also the two farms to the north that he had recently purchased. Richard recalls that:

> *Dr. Truesdale had a plan to raise beef for the hospital. He bought these registered Aberdeen Angus cattle and bred them. I don't remember how many there were, between a dozen and two dozen, maybe. Dad had a hired hand, one of the Wood boys from Pottersville. I think it was Raymond Wood that used to help around.*

One of Raymond Bixby's first tasks was to update the Head House to 1945 standards. Once the house was wired for electricity and indoor plumbing was installed, Bixby moved his wife Barbara and two children Dick and Marjory from their home in Long Highway's former Number 9 Schoolhouse to Goosewing Farm. However, within weeks of the Bixbys' move Dr. Truesdale died of a heart attack. The Truesdale family instructed Raymond to sell off the cattle and wind down the farming operation. It took a year and half, and when the work was done the Bixby family moved back to Long Highway.

Dick Bixby recalls their time at Goosewing Farm fondly. His favorite farm vehicle was a giant World War II Jeep-like truck with canvas sides and four-wheel-drive. It was perfect for farm work and charging through the snow. At Christmastime the family decorated it with jingle bells and drove it to the party at the Odd Fellows Hall singing all the way.

Dick also remembers the Hutchinson family still spending summers on the farm but now renting the larger Sisson House instead of the Head House.

My sister Marjory had, in the summer, the Hutchinson girl to play with. I remember crawling up the hay mound with field glasses and watching the ships go by out there near Cuttyhunk. I remember going fishing and playing on the beach a lot. We'd play with my cousin Walter Elwell.

Dick's mother was responsible for collecting the parking fees from beachgoers.

I remember her being terribly upset because someone had the nerve to hand her a twenty dollar bill with the presumption that she wouldn't have the change!

Like Don Truchon, Dick Bixby's memories of the Sisson Family and Goosewing Farm are connected to World War II.

I remember as a little kid going with my folks to Tom Sisson's house. They had spread this map out on the coffee table in the living room. My folks and Tom and his wife were pouring over the map trying to understand where Pearl Harbor, Hawaii was. This was on December 7, 1941. I also remember being in the Head House hearing of VJ Day, the end of World War II. I guess I was ten. It was 1945.[22]

THE WILDES FAMILY

With Dr. Truesdale's cattle business dissolved, Merrick and Hilda Wildes came to the property as tenant farmers in 1946 and settled into the Head House. The Wildes had four children, Meredith, Emerson, Everett and Susan. Meredith remembers one especially cold winter in the 1960s when Tunipus Pond froze solid. Her father made the best of the weather and created a shortcut by driving his John Deere tractor with a trailer filled with silage right across the pond and then on to the Shaw Farm on

Merrick and Emerson Wildes at the Goosewing Barn, c. 1950. Courtesy of the Wildes Family

Shaw Road. Mrs. Wildes (like her predecessor Mrs. Bixby) collected parking fees from beach-goers for many years. The Wildes boys were especially involved in the work of the farm, and the family continued to run a dairy farm at Goosewing until 1990.

THE ACEBES FAMILY

Among the Truesdale family's summer renters were Carl and Carol Acebes, who first visited Goosewing Farm in 1974 and later with their two children Calyn and Rowan. In the 1980s the Truesdale Trust agreed to sell its Goosewing Beach property to The Nature Conservancy and the Goosewing Beach Nature Preserve was organized to protect the barrier beach and adjacent Quicksand Pond ecosystem, including the endangered Piper Plovers.

In 1992, the Truesdale Trust sold the 60.4 acre Goosewing Farm to the Acebes family. The farm's entire waterfront is under a conservation easement and the farm is restricted to five residences.[23] The Acebes family implemented a master plan for the farm that had as its goals the historic preservation and reconstruction of the property's buildings as well as the rejuvenation of this traditional Little Compton farm. The plan included replacing asphalt laneways with gravel, burying overhead utility lines, and completing a historically accurate restoration of the Head House. The

The Acebes Family at Goosewing Farm, 1999. Courtesy of Carl and Carol Acebes.

project has been led by award-winning architect, Peter Q. Bohlin, Bohlin Cywinski Jackson. Bohlin was named the American Institute of Architects' 2010 Gold Medal winner (the highest honor bestowed annually to an American architect by that the organization).

In 2012, the Acebes family placed Goosewing Farm in a family perpetual trust to ensure the historic buildings and landscape will remain undisturbed and preserved for future generations and the over 300 year history as a working farm continues uninterrupted.

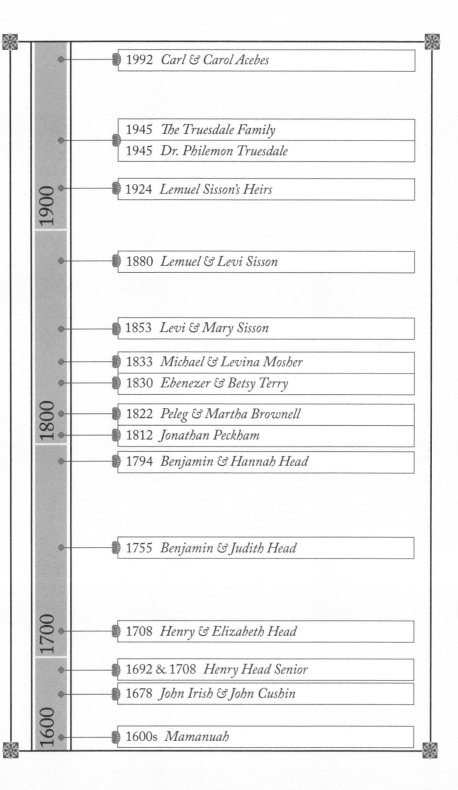

1992 *Carl & Carol Acebes*

1945 *The Truesdale Family*
1945 *Dr. Philemon Truesdale*

1924 *Lemuel Sisson's Heirs*

1900

1880 *Lemuel & Levi Sisson*

1853 *Levi & Mary Sisson*

1833 *Michael & Levina Mosher*

1830 *Ebenezer & Betsy Terry*

1822 *Peleg & Martha Brownell*

1812 *Jonathan Peckham*

1794 *Benjamin & Hannah Head*

1800

1755 *Benjamin & Judith Head*

1708 *Henry & Elizabeth Head*

1700

1692 & 1708 *Henry Head Senior*

1678 *John Irish & John Cushin*

1600

1600s *Mamanuah*

The Number 4 School House. *Photo by Bart Brownell.*

The Number 4 Schoolhouse

HAPPY DAYS

By Jillian Jennett & Marjory O'Toole

The Number 4 Schoolhouse is now a comfortable private home located on West Main Road. As its name implies it was once one of the ten District Schoolhouses that provided Little Compton's children with an eighth-grade education. When the centralized Josephine F. Wilbur School opened on the Commons in 1929, the town sold its one-room schoolhouses, and Number 4 began its second life as a home. Present-day owners Susan Sorrentino and John Lewis display a c. 1910 photograph of the school building with its students lined up in front. The teacher, Miss Sullivan, had written "Happy Days" on the reverse. It was her first class. The photo caption reminds us that despite the overcrowding, rapid teacher turnover, and the sometimes poor condition of the school reported by a series of annual reports, the Number 4 Schoolhouse was a happy place for its teachers and students. Today Susan and John call their home "Happy Days" in honor of the school and everyone who taught or studied there.

THE BROWN FARM

Before the property was a schoolhouse lot, it was farmland that passed through several generations of the Brown family. Tobias Brown of Portsmouth and Tiverton acquired large tracts of land in Little Compton and distributed them to two of his sons at his death in 1734. Both boys were probably living and farming in Little Compton long before that date. Son Robert was given the family's northernmost land stretching across both sides of the "highway" or West Main Road.[1] A small portion of that land on the east of the highway would one day become the schoolhouse lot. Robert ran a farm that raised cattle and sheep. When he passed in 1791 he left all of his real estate to his only son Moses and required him to provide a home to his sisters Alice and Elizabeth. Regarding Elizabeth, Robert wrote that Moses:

> *is to find her as much flax and wool as she can spin herself and he is to pay the weaving of it for her as long as she remains unmarried and my house is to be her home until she is of age or married and when she is at age or married she shall have fifteen pounds of flax and twenty pounds of wool.*

Moses was to provide her a "home and victuals" and to allow her to "work for herself" meaning that any money she earned from her spinning was hers to keep. Elizabeth may have been taught to read, but it is unlikely that she ever attended school. Girls of that time were taught all they needed to know to run a household and to weave and spin by the older women in their lives. Robert named Moses and his "well beloved friend and neighbor John Hunt" executors of his will.[2] The Hunts would continue their neighborly care of the Browns into the next generation.

CHARGEABLE TO THE TOWN

Moses' ownership of the property was filled with strife. Beginning in 1817 Moses and his sons Abraham, Robert and Abner appear repeatedly in the town records due to their inability, or perceived inability, to manage their own affairs. Because of complaints from neighbors, the town frequently stepped in assigning guardians to supervise the Browns' spending and land management.

Why would neighbors care about the Brown's private affairs? If the Browns mismanaged their property and were unable to care for themselves, they would have become "chargeable" to the town. The town would have been obligated to support them, and this meant higher taxes for everyone in Little Compton. Both residents and town officials kept a watchful eye on their neighbors to prevent this from happening and to keep taxes as low as possible.

Numerous town records from the eighteenth and nineteenth centuries deal with just this issue. Dozens of Little Compton families and individuals

lived on the edge of poverty. To prevent people from becoming chargeable, the town would provide guardians to help manage their estates, order
the indenture of their children so they would work for their room and
board, or in the case of non-residents "order them out" of Little Compton
back to the towns of their birth. Each of these steps was an effort to keep
the poor sheltered and fed while minimizing the financial burden on the
town's other residents.

The Browns were a particularly troublesome case. On January 1,
1817 Little Compton's Probate Court declared Moses and his three sons
all "Non-compis Mentis…Incapable of managing their affairs and
consequently liable to become chargeable to sd Town." Isaac and Pardon
Brownell were appointed their guardians, but the Browns continued to
struggle.[3] Between 1817 and 1842 the Browns appear numerous times in
the records, appealing the Probate Court's decisions, being released from
their guardianships, then receiving more complaints and being assigned
guardians over and over again.[4] The Overseers of the Poor "bound out" or
indentured Abraham's son William in 1824, meaning that he was ordered
to work for another family until he was twenty-one years old in exchange
for food, shelter, clothing and an education.[5] William had no choice
but to accept the indenture, and he would have been punished if he left
it before his twenty-first birthday.

Robert Brown purchased the land containing the future schoolhouse
lot from his father Moses in 1808 for $1,000.[6] Robert was the most
successful of the Brown men in petitioning the Probate Court to appeal
the complaints against him and release his guardianships. Even so Robert,
who was called both a "spendthrift" and "intemperate" in the records, was
frequently under the control of guardians.[7] Benjamin Hunt's guardianship
began in 1826. Among other things the Hunts began to care for Robert's
son Frederick who began to use the last name Hunt instead of Brown.[8]
Benjamin Hunt was ordered by Probate Officials to inventory Robert's
estate, and Hunt requested permission from the State General Assembly
to begin selling Robert's land to pay his debts. Permission was granted.[9]
Selling land was a last resort for Little Compton families to ward off
poverty. Doing so helped Robert support himself, but unlike so many
other local fathers at his death, he had no land left to leave to his children.

Robert Brown lived constantly under the watchful eyes of town officials, though his guardians changed over time. In 1842 Brown and his guardian Nathaniel Church signed a document with the trustees for the local School District to lease the schoolhouse lot to them.

We the abovesaid Brown & Church, have let and leased to the abovesaid Benjamin Grinnell, William Howland, John B Howland and Humphrey Brown [a lot of land] three rods long north and three rods long East from the south west corner of said Brown and called the Old Orchard joining Job Seabury's land, for the consideration of 10 cents a year to set a School-House on, so long as they the said Grinnell, Howlands and Brown or their heirs or assigns shall keep the School-House in repair and keep a School in it, short seasons excepted…the manure made from the said School House to be left there for the benefits of the farm.

EARLY SCHOOLS

This was the beginning of Schoolhouse Number 4. Originally the school building for District 3, the building was later renamed District 4 when the two districts combined in the late 1880s. The school was built shortly after 1842 and remained in use through 1929.

As in many New England towns Little Compton's town fathers were keen on providing educational opportunities to the local youth. Less than a decade after the first English families moved to Little Compton, the

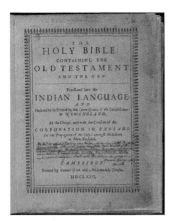

The American Indian Bible.

Town Selectmen hired Nathaniel Searles as the first schoolmaster in 1688. A number of different men filled the annual position in those early years, and the selectmen spent a great deal of time searching for appropriate teachers in Newport and Boston.

There were also two Indian Schools in seventeenth-century Little Compton focused on teaching Native People of all ages to read the Bible. In 1693 traveling ministers reported with pride on the progress being made educating Little Compton's Indians. Ten Indians could read the Bible and several more their catechism. In addition to two Indian preachers there was also an Indian schoolmaster named Aham.[11]

In the early years, sometimes the town paid for school – sometimes parents paid. At times they shared the expense, as in 1702 when Jonathan Head was schoolmaster and the Town Council voted:

> *They that send their children to school shall pay 4 p for every writing scholar and 2 p per week for a reading scholar and the remainder of the money to be paid by the town to make up the ten pounds.*

In part because of the expense, eighteenth-century girls were often taught just to read while boys were taught to read and write. Later arithmetic was added to the curriculum, and by the nineteenth century girls and boys were receiving a more well-rounded education.

Before designated school buildings were constructed, teachers moved three or four times each year to teach in private homes in different neighborhoods. Residents determined where these schools would be located, in essence establishing the first informal school districts and school district committees. An early school operated out of the Town Meeting House on the Commons, and the first specific school building, Peaked Top, was built in 1725. Peaked Top School was moved to at least three different locations during its lifetime.[12]

The number and location of schools and school districts changed with the changing needs of Little Compton's families, but the school district system, and neighborhood control of the schools, continued until 1929 when the Wilbur School was built. In 1828 the State of Rhode Island stepped in and ruled that every town establish formal school districts and build a school in each district. It was at this time that the state started sending education funding to its cities and towns and public education through grade eight became fully free. Little Compton had nine school districts in 1844, ten in 1870 and less in the early-twentieth century.

SCHOOLHOUSE NUMBER 4

Schoolhouse Number 4 appears in a variety of town records that help us understand its chain of ownership and its daily operations as a school. Farmer John B. Howland acquired the schoolhouse lot from Robert Brown

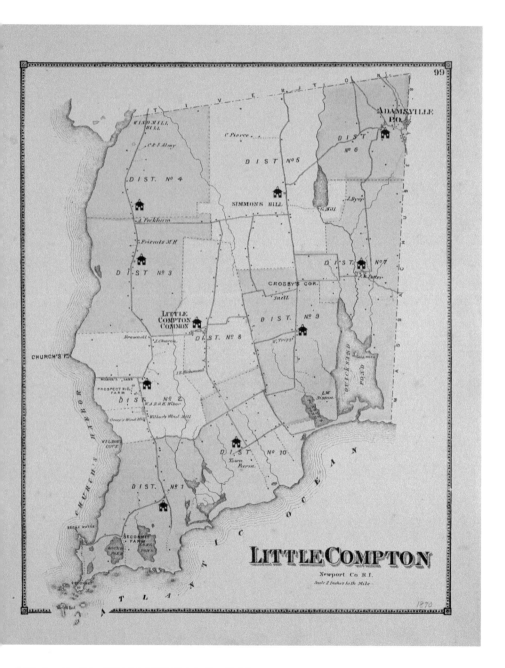

Little Compton School Districts, 1870. Map by Tom Callahan.

and left it to his son Edward Howland in 1871. Like the Browns, Edward Howland found himself in some financial difficulty that put his land at risk. In 1894 the local sheriff seized sixteen different properties belonging to Edward Howland and sold them at public auction in order to pay debts resulting from a law suit. One of those properties was the Number 4 Schoolhouse lot, another was the Peleg Bailey Farm also described in this book. The Town of Little Compton purchased the Number 4 Schoolhouse lot with a high bid of $100 at the auction that took place on the Town Hall steps.[13]

Like all of Little Compton's District Schools the Number 4 School offered a Summer, Winter and Spring Term to Little Compton's boys and girls. In 1885 the school sat in the center of what was then called District Number 3. It had a total of fourteen students, and an average daily attendance of ten. What was then called District Number Four was located just to the north and reached to the Tiverton line. Its even lower attendance averaged only seven students per day. In District Three the Summer Term lasted one hundred days, the Winter Term lasted sixty days and the Spring Term was a brief twenty days. The total number of school days offered was often close to 180 but varied from year to year as the school was sometimes closed for bad weather, muddy roads, or outbreaks of measles, scarlet fever, or influenza.[14] The school schedule had no Fall Term and only the briefest of Spring Terms, clearly revolving around the needs of local farming families, allowing the students plenty of time to help with agricultural work.[15]

Teacher turnover was common and finding qualified teachers was a constant challenge for the district's trustees. Teachers would leave to get married, to take a better job, or due to illness. The 1885 School Report mentions one teacher's passing and notes that she was able to stay at the school for almost three years, a long stretch at that time:

A shadow of the deepest gloom has been cast over our community and especially over the field covered by the report of the superintendent, by the sudden death of Miss Lillian R. Almy, a teacher of District No. 3. In the spring of 1882, Miss Almy was secured as a teacher for this district.

Special Rules and Regulations for the Government of the Public Schools in the Town of Little Compton – 1897

1. Schools to be opened at nine o'clock in the morning and to consist of two sessions of three hours each, with an intermission of not less than one hour.

2. Each scholar shall be entitled to a recess of fifteen minutes. Provided, that if the order or discipline of the school requires it, the teacher may cause any scholar to have his recess alone.

3. The government and discipline of the school shall be of a mild and parental character, the teacher shall endeavor by mild measures to bring the scholars to obedience, when corporal punishment is necessary it shall be inflicted with judgement and discretion.

4. The teachers shall have control of the scholars from the time they come upon the school grounds until they leave the same.

5. Teachers are allowed one-half day in each term for visiting other schools.

6. Smoking or chewing tobacco upon the school premises strictly forbidden.

7. Any scholar who is found guilty of incorrigibly bad conduct or violation of school regulations may be expelled from school (not readmitted without consent of the school committee.)

8. Every pupil who shall, on or around the school premises, use or write any profane or unchaste language, or shall draw or cut any obscene picture or representation, shall be excluded from the school.

9. Any scholar who is found guilty of defacing school buildings must be reported to parents and school committee. (Teacher responsible.)

10. Any scholar willfully destroying or injuring school books or other school supplies must be reported to parents and school committee. (Teacher responsible.)

11. Teachers may allow books to be taken home if they think it is best to do so. Parents must be responsible for injury or loss.

12. Teachers must keep books neatly covered.

13. Orders for school supplies must be endorsed by some member of School Committee or Superintendent of Schools.

14. Playgrounds must be limited by teacher and strict obedience to the regulation enforced. No pupil shall be allowed to leave the same without consent of teacher.

15. Teachers will be held responsible for the prompt and efficient enforcement of the above rules.

This was her first attempt at teaching and she continued in the same school until her fatal illness, making nearly three years' successive in teaching.[16]

Sometime between 1886 and 1890 the district trustees decided to merge Districts 3 and 4. The original Number 4 Schoolhouse to the north was abandoned and eventually taken down.[17] The Number 3 Schoolhouse to the south was renamed Number 4 and is the subject of this history.

The district merger solved the problem of low attendance at the two schools but left parents and school officials unhappy regarding the condition of the school and the distance some students had to travel. In 1892 the Superintendent of Schools reported that:

District No. 4 is sadly in need of a school-house and we would recommend that before another year shall have passed, measures may be taken towards erecting a building which shall be centrally located and more deserving the name of a school-house than the one now occupied.

The house in District No. 4 was made more comfortable for cold weather, during the autumn, but a new building is greatly needed.

The school had different teachers almost every year. Miss Edna May Hambly was responsible for the school in 1896-7 and for several subsequent years. The consistency paid off. The 1899 school report stated:

Nos. 4 and 7, in which there has been no change of teachers for the year, having had no break in the regular routine work, have had greater opportunity for advancement than any other schools.[20]

There was more good news for Miss Hambly and the families of District Number 4 in 1901:

Very notable progress has been made at No. 4 during the year. Miss Hambly taught with her usual success the Spring and Fall terms, and

Edna May Hambly, Teacher, Schoolhouse Number 4. *Courtesy of Donald Gomez.*

then it was thought best to place her in school No. 9. On short notice we were fortunate in securing the services of Miss Eva L. Swift, a teacher of experience and ability, and one who takes a lively interest in each pupil and the work generally. She is progressive, second to none in her efforts to obtain the best results possible.

I am very glad to note here that in looking over the register of this school I find 20 pupils enrolled and but five tardy marks recorded over the last four months, and but few absences compared with other schools in town. The parents in this district seem to appreciate the value of punctuality and regular attendance.[21]

Enrollment at Number 4 Schoolhouse gradually increased over time, and school officials oversaw small improvements like the installation of new blackboards and repositioned seats and desks in 1905.[22] The Progressive Education Movement was growing throughout America and concerned citizens were paying more attention to local students' surroundings. By 1907 Number 4 was one of the two largest schools in Little Compton with thirty-two students. The Superintendent wrote:

No. 4 has been crowded all year and at present writing it would seem that several new pupils will come in the Fall term. We may be called upon to enlarge the building.[23]

By 1909 school crowding was a widespread problem and local reformers like Josephine F. Wilbur began to lobby for the construction of a new, modern, central school on the Commons. At first their efforts were to no avail. Again, the Superintendent wrote about less than ideal conditions:

Numbers One, Two, and Four are too small to accommodate the children in these sections and are too crowded for the good of the children both physically and mentally. The condition is not so serious in the summer with open windows and doors, as in winter with everything closed and a hot fire in the center of the room, overheating those sitting nearby while others more remote are not any too warm. In passing, it seems to me it would be well to have a metallic screen for each stove, thereby

Number 4 Schoolhouse, c. 1910. The current owners found a copy of this photograph with "Happy Days" written across the back. Postcard by O.E. Dubois. LCHS Collection.

securing a better circulation of air, and protecting from the direct rays of heat the scholars near it.

Some dissatisfaction has been expressed on account of the location of Number Four. It is not centrally located for that part of the town, as there is only one family sending children to that school living south of it, about one-eighth of a mile away; while some to the north live about two miles from it. This of course is too far for any child to walk to and from school every day and either transportation ought to be furnished or a more central location secured.[24]

And in 1912:

Schools Numbers one, two, and four have been in very bad shape for good work, on account of crowded conditions that have been unavoidable. School buildings two and four should be enlarged for the accommodation of these growing districts. The desks in Number Four are not fit for use and should be thrown out and new ones installed in their places.[25]

Enrollment hovered around forty students from 1914 to 1924 and reached an all-time high of fifty-five students in 1920.[26] Around 1915 the town began offering public transportation to and from the one-room schools. This enabled educators to grade some of the schools since every child in the neighborhood no longer had to walk to the same school building. Number 4 School was used for the younger grades. The Little Compton Historical Society's Executive Director of fifty years, Carlton Brownell attended the school and shared his memories with the current owners. Other Little Compton residents can still remember their time there.

I remember every school had a stove. When you got there it was so cold, the teacher would have you run around the room until it got warm. They had a pile of wood out back, the teacher had to put in the wood. It was a flat stove, so everyone brought a jar of cocoa or something and put it on the stove. – Virginia Bullock Watt[27]

Josephine Wilbur passed away at an early age in 1923. It was after her death that local people actively took up the cause of a central school for Little Compton. In 1924 they invited officials from the State Board of Education to tour the town's schools and report on their findings.

The official report found all of Little Compton's one room schools lacking. It reported that in 1924 the Number 4 Schoolhouse was used for grades one, two and three and had a total of forty-eight students, forty of whom arrived by bus.

Schoolhouse No. 4, a frame building, a small part of which is new, the structure having been enlarged recently, is located beside the main state highway. The roof is shingled and does not leak, but the sides admit rainwater in wet weather. The older part of the building is in poor condition. The floor is good. Blackboards are of painted wood, and worn. School textbooks are generally dilapidated; few additional books for reading by the primary pupils of the first three grades attending this school have been provided.

The school is generally deficient in wholesome sanitary standards. The lighting, from windows on both sides, does not conform to the accepted

Form 6

Book and Supply Report of   Town of *Little Compton, R.I.*   School, *District No. 4.*

For term ending *June 27,*   *1924*

	Arithmetic, Written	" Elementary	" Mental	Civics	Geography, G.S.	" Primary	Grammar	History, U.S.	Language, Part I	" Part II	Music Reader, No. 1	" No. 2	Physiology, Lar e	" Small	5th Readers	4th	3rd	2nd	1st	Primers	Spellers	Writing Books, No. 1	" No. 2	" No. 3	" No. 4	" No. 5	" No. 6	Drawing Books, No. 1	" No. 2	" No. 3	" No. 4	Crayons	Erasers	Lead Pencils	Ink	Penholders	Pens
1. On hand as per last report																																					
2. Received during the term																																					
3. Total																																					
4. Lost or worn out																																					
5. Remaining on hand	23			11		17	22							3		33/15	52	24											2C long 24	27		28	1/2				

This return is to be made out in Duplicate by the Principal of every school; one copy to be sent to the Superintendent of Public Schools, and one copy retained b

Number 4 School Book & Supply Report, 1924. LCHS Collection.

one-direction standard, and, besides, is insufficient as measured by relation of glazed area to floor area. Floor area and cubic measurement are inadequate. The heating plant, unjacketed wood stove, is not sufficient to keep the building warm, and there is no provision for maintaining even temperature. No thermometer was provided; the school clock does not keep time.

There is no well on the premises, and no other provision is made for drinking water or for water for washing hands. Such water as is used is obtained from an open dug well on a neighboring farm.

Separate outbuildings are provided, but these are not kept clean, and the walls are mutilated. Neither house is screened, and the approaches do not conform to decent standards. In warm weather, these buildings constitute a nuisance; and in cold weather the exposure involved in use constitutes a danger to the general health of the young children who attend the school.[28]

With similarly discouraging reports for each of the schools in town, local voters agreed to build a single central school on the Commons for grades one to twelve. When the Josephine F. Wilbur School opened in September 1929 Little Compton's one-room schools were officially out of business. The Number 4 Schoolhouse began a new chapter as a home.

A HAPPY HOME

Once again the schoolhouse was for sale at public auction, this time with all of the town's one-room schools. Hetty Newton, an across-the-street neighbor, was the high bidder for Number 4 and purchased the property for $710.[29] Mrs. Newton rented the property to the Hargraves family. Barbara Passmore, who lives nearby the Schoolhouse, remembers going to the Hargraves to play with their five children when she was a little girl. The family of seven lived together in one large room, exactly as the building had been used as a school. Nina Hargraves hung fabric drapes from the ceiling to divide the large space into separate rooms. Barbara remembers that Raymond Hargraves fished for a living. In the 1940 Federal Census Raymond reported that he was a farm laborer who worked eighty-four hours a week to support his growing family. Their rent was $10 a month.[30]

Mrs. Newton sold the Schoolhouse to William Dennis in 1951 who owned the property until 1957.[31] Barbara Passmore remembers several renters at this time including June Cavaca Bento and Gail and John Rocha. Retired Marine Clayton Lester and his first wife Adele purchased the property in 1957 and lived there for many years.[32] Like many retired men in Little Compton, Clayton worked part-time on one of the town's large properties. He worked as a gardener for the Whitins who lived across the street from the Schoolhouse. Clayton and his second wife Mildred sold the house to David and Polly Emilita in 1991, a young couple who enjoyed the Schoolhouse as a starter home before moving to Westport.[33] Maureen Anderson, a registered nurse, became the Schoolhouse's next owner in 1997 and in turn sold to John Lewis and Susan Sorrentino in 2004, the current owners. Barbara Passmore remembers each of the Schoolhouse residents as "amiable" people and welcome additions to the neighborhood.

Each owner made changes and improvements to Schoolhouse Number 4 moving it through a transition from a nineteenth-century schoolhouse to an expanded, comfortable, twenty-first century home. The exterior of the main portion of the house still clearly resembles a classic New England schoolhouse, but the well-designed interior invites visitors to enjoy all the comforts of home.

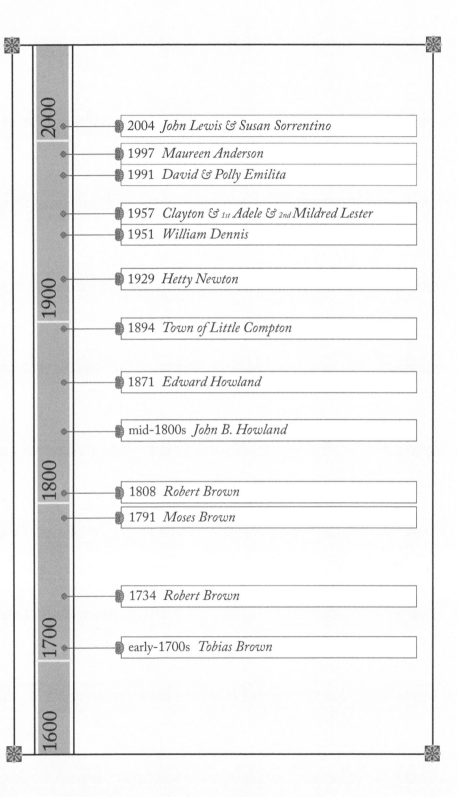

2000

2004 *John Lewis & Susan Sorrentino*

1997 *Maureen Anderson*

1991 *David & Polly Emilita*

1957 *Clayton & 1st Adele & 2nd Mildred Lester*

1951 *William Dennis*

1929 *Hetty Newton*

1900

1894 *Town of Little Compton*

1871 *Edward Howland*

mid-1800s *John B. Howland*

1800

1808 *Robert Brown*

1791 *Moses Brown*

1734 *Robert Brown*

1700

early-1700s *Tobias Brown*

1600

Little Compton Town Vault.

Afterword

RESEARCH THE HISTORY OF YOUR OWN LITTLE COMPTON HOUSE

By Marian Pierre-Louis

Now that you've reached the end of this publication, you are probably enjoying the warm glow that comes from diving into the history of your favorite place on earth. Hopefully the preceding house histories have intrigued you, perhaps even made you curious to learn more about Little Compton history and about your own house. The following essay will encourage and inspire you to research the history of your own Little Compton house.

How old does my house have to be?

People have different ideas about how old houses have to be before you can or should research them. Many folks conjure up images of beautiful colonials from the 1700s. While those do make for interesting stories, any house can be researched, even modern ones. The difference will be how long the process will take you and the amount of information you find. Newer houses will obviously be quicker to research, but you will find less information. Old houses will provide a trove of information but the research could keep you going for years.

What houses am I allowed to research?

You are, of course, allowed to research the history of your own house. Many people wonder if it's permissible to research the history of other people's houses. Maybe you'd like to research the history of the summer house you stayed in as a child. The fact is, house history research is based on public record. As such, you are free to research any house you like. The records you will use are publicly available. Most people don't have the time or interest to research other people's houses but local historians often research historic houses within their town in order to preserve the history. If you do research your own house or someone else's, please consider sharing what you find with the Little Compton History Society so that they will be able to preserve that information for all time.

Getting Started

Before you really dive into house history research do these two exercises. They will get you in the mood and will provide a baseline so that you can see just how far you have come when you finish.

1) Document your house now

The first exercise involves documenting your house the way it is right now. Grab a camera or a smart phone and head outside. Photograph your house from all different sides. Take some photos from the corners so that you can see two sides at one time. If you have interesting architectural details zoom in to get close-ups of those. Next photograph your property. You can probably take just a few shots that encompass your whole lot but be sure to get both front and back. If you have any outbuildings such as barns or sheds, photograph those separately. And be sure to document any physical structures such as stone walls, wells, docks or other items that might be on your property.

Next head inside. Photograph every room you have. Take photos that show the whole room. You may have to take it from several angles. Then, again, pay attention to the details. If you have significant interior features such as fireplaces, wood beams, old doorknob hardware or hand carved details be sure to photograph those separately.

The purpose of photographing your house is that it becomes part of your house history document. You may regard it simply as the place where you live right now, but in a matter of five years your house, inside and out, could look very different. By documenting your house right now you will always be able to refer back to how the house looked in 2015.

2) Take a stroll

Take a stroll through the Old Commons Burial Ground in the center of Little Compton. You can take your camera if you like. The idea is not to look for anything in particular but pass the grounds and take notice of the shape, condition and age of the gravestones. Most importantly take notice of the surnames that appear on the gravestones. Unless you are very familiar with Little Compton history, the names will likely not mean anything to you. Mentally make note of which names are very prevalent and during which time periods. In this way you will start to become familiar with the families that founded and built the town over the centuries.

As you proceed with your house history research you will learn the individual surnames of the families that lived in your home. While doing so, you may recall the day you took that stroll in the cemetery and viewed the names before.

Toward the end of your research, take another stroll through the cemetery. This time look specifically for gravestones of the families that lived in your house. You will feel a connection, even privilege, of having discovered the former residents of your home.

Little Compton, as is typical in much of Rhode Island, has many small cemeteries. In fact there are over forty cemeteries in town. You don't need to visit them all, but do make note of any small cemeteries that are located in the vicinity of your house. These may be family plots for former residents of your house, and it would be worthwhile discovering their location.

If you don't see any cemeteries nearby but you are still curious, then visit the Rhode Island Historical Cemetery Commission website (http://www.rihistoriccemeteries.org) to find the name and specific location of cemeteries in Little Compton or explore the Historical Society's Cemetery Index available on their website (littlecompton.org) under Historical Resources.

Now that you've set the stage, it's time to dig into house history research.

Start with the Deeds

It's very important to start house history research by searching for the deeds themselves. Some people think that they can search for information simply using their address. The fact is that as you go back in time the street number of your house may have changed and the name of your street may have changed as well. Also, many records over a century ago were recorded by the owner's last name rather than the address. By doing deed research first you will gather the names of all the previous owners of your house and from there you will be in a good position to complete the rest of your research no matter how it is sorted.

Finding Your Current Deed

The information you need to start is the book and page number of your current deed. If you have your deed handy in your home files then you can simply look at it to get the information. If you don't know where the deed to your house is, there is another solution. You need to access the Little Compton Assessor's information online. You can access this in two ways: go to the town of Little Compton website at http://www.little-compton.com and visit the assessor's page under departments, Town Boards. From there look for the "Vision Online Database." Or you can go to the database directly at http://gis.vgsi.com/LittleComptonRI. Within the database search by address or owner and pull up your property information. You will find the book and page number on the resulting page.

The assessor's database summary for your property may also include previous sales of your house. Be sure to jot this information down. Also, be on the lookout for the "Year Built." The year may not be completely accurate but at least it will give you an idea of when your house was built.

Chaining a Deed

When doing deed research it is helpful to make a chart. You can find free downloadable sample charts in MS Word (editable) and PDF format at the New England House Historian blog (http://nehousehistorian.blogspot.com/2010/09/using-deed-chart-to-trace-your-deeds.html).

Enter your existing deed's book and page number on the chart and enter your name in the Grantee column. Put the name(s) of the person who sold you your house in the grantor column and then fill out the rest of the information. Sale price information is available for modern deeds but be aware that as you go back in time it is less likely that this information will be recorded.

You will need to go to the Little Compton Town Hall to complete the rest of your deed research. In your current deed, right after the land description, you will likely find a reference to the previous deed's book and page number. This is the next deed you need to look at.

Deed Index Books. Little Compton Town Vault.

The deeds in Town Hall are recorded in Books (Volumes). More modern deeds have a single year in a single volume. Older deeds group multiple years. Pull the book that matches the book you have listed on your deed chart and find your way to the correct page.

The next deed you pull will be for the person who sold you your house (the grantor) when they were a grantee (buying the house). Next you will write the name of their grantor (the person who sold them the house). Then make sure to look beyond the description to the book and page reference for the deed before that.

This process is called "chaining a deed." In most cases each person on your chart will be listed twice - once as the grantee (when they bought the house) and once as the grantor (when they sold the house). Continue in this way as far back as possible, inching closer to the year you think your house was built.

If you encounter deeds that do not provide a previous book and page reference then you will need to access the index books. You will find these in the lower right hand back corner of the Town Hall vault. Search for the last known owner alphabetically by surname. You will find entries in the index books for both Grantors and Grantees. Once you locate the correct name, ensure that you have the correct location in case the previous owner bought multiple properties in Little Compton during the course of their life. Once you have found the correct listing, note the book and page number on your deed chart. Next find the book that contains the new reference and locate the deed. It's a slower process using the indexes but it is invaluable when you don't have a book and page reference to help you go to a deed directly.

Researching the deeds to your house can take quite awhile, but the reward will be great as it will allow you to continue on with your research in a much easier fashion.

Previous Home Owners in the Census Records

Now you are in a position to start learning about previous home owners. The best place to start is with US Federal Census records. Census records are available every ten years from 1790 to (currently) 1940. However, the 1890 census is not available due to destruction of the records. Census records are available online for free from FamilySearch.org and with a pay subscription from Ancestry.com. Most libraries have Ancestry.com available for free from within the library (no home access). Ancestry.com is the only website that has all census records.

From 1850 to the present, the censuses recorded every person in each household individually by name. Prior to 1850 only the head of household is listed with slash marks indicating how many other people lived in the house. These are still helpful, particularly if you have a very old house.

As each census draws closer to the present it provides more detailed information. Typical information you will find on a census includes age, marital status, race, place of birth, parents' place of birth, occupation, whether naturalized and much more. You can learn quite a bit from the census records, and the information will help you see the previous owners of your house as real people with stories of their own.

Check each census to locate the previous owners of your home from 1940 back as far as the known date of your house (to 1790). Be aware, especially in a summer community like Little Compton, that the owners of homes may not have lived in their Little Compton home except during the summer time. This is most likely for twentieth-century residents. For that reason you may find the previous owners listed in the censuses in their winter homes in another state. This may make your research a little more challenging. This means that when you search the census records for the names of the previous owners you will not find your house in Little Compton. To make things more complicated renters may be listed in the house. Without knowing their names in advance it will be harder to find them in the censuses. In this case, you can use other records, such as city directories to discover the names of the renters.

Other Records at Town Hall

There are other useful records at Town Hall that will be easier to use once you complete the census research. You will need to provide information to the staff in the Town Clerk's office to access Vital Record and Probate information.

Vital records are critical for getting a full view of the families that lived in your home. One hundred years ago life expectancy and infant mortality was not what it is today. Children may have been born and died in the years between census enumeration. Vital records – births, marriages and deaths – will help fill in these gaps. You can access these records at Town Hall but you also have some online options. Vital records were compiled by James N. Arnold in a publication called *Vital Records of Rhode Island, 1636-1850*. You can find the publication in book form at libraries, in digitized form online at the (free, non-searchable) InternetArchive.com or in digitized and searchable format on Ancestry.com.

Probate records, while potentially more complex to look at, can provide detailed information about the families who lived in your home. Probated wills and administration files will piece together information about the families and their relationships. One little known document, however, is particularly rich for house historians. Probated estates typically held estate or house inventory documents. These were a listing of the contents of each house taken after the death of the homeowner. The inventories can be quite detailed and provide information not only about the owners but may list objects that are still found in your home, particularly if it has been in the same family for many generations. These records, which can be found all the way back to the 1600s, can provide information about the owner's economic status, occupation and level of education based on the items that are listed as being found in the house. Probate records are most easily accessed from Town Hall though they are available in microfilm format from the Family History Library in Salt Lake City (see familysearch.org for information on how to access microfilm locally anywhere in the United States).

Rhode Island Historical Preservation & Heritage Commission

The Rhode Island Historical Preservation & Heritage Commission operates a statewide historical preservation program that inventories historic buildings and sites. They have published a guide called *Historic and Architectural Resources of Little Compton, Rhode Island (1990)*. It can be found online at http://www.preservation.ri.gov/pdfs_zips_downloads/survey_pdfs/little_compton.pdf. This guide may provide a passing mention of your house or detailed information so it is worth a look. It also includes photographs.

Other resources

Other resources that will help you with your house history research include historical newspapers, historical maps, tax records, historical photographs, and Rhode Island state census records. You can find these records online at Ancestry.com, the Library of Congress (loc.gov) or offline at the Little Compton Historical Society or the Rhode Island Historical Society.

Know Your History!

One of the unique aspects of Little Compton history is that prior to 1747 it was a part of Massachusetts. If your house is older than 1747 you will have to search in Massachusetts for documents relating to your house. From 1685 to 1746 you will search Bristol County, Massachusetts records. Prior to 1685 you will need to search Plymouth Colony records.

Local History Resources

Take advantage of the wealth of historical information about Little Compton that is already in print. These histories or manuscripts may contain reference to your house or to the families that lived in them. Also, be sure to access the oral history archive (as well as other resources) located at the Little Compton Historical Society.

Below is a select list of resources for Little Compton history. Check the Ocean State Libraries catalog for further resources.

- Cemetery Transcriptions, unpublished typescript. Found at the Brownell Public Library.
- Lisle, Janet. *The History of Little Compton: First Light Sakonnet 1660-1820.* Little Compton, RI: Little Compton Historical Society, 2010.
- Lisle, Janet. *The History of Little Compton: A Home By the Sea 1820-1950.* Little Compton, RI: Little Compton Historical Society, 2012.
- *Remembering Adamsville: Oral Histories Collected by the Little Compton Historical Society.* Little Compton, RI: Little Compton Historical Society, 2013.
- *Three Centuries: Little Compton Tercentennial, 1675-1975.*
- Wilbour, Sarah Soule. *Diaries from 1882-1891.* These published diaries mention many Little Compton residents and homes during that time period.

When you've completed your house history research please consider sharing a copy of some or all of it with the Little Compton Historical Society so that they may preserve your history of your house.

For more general information about house history research view the New England House Historian blog online at http://nehousehistorian. blogspot.com. Also, look for the book *House Histories: A Guide to Tracing the Genealogy of Your House* by Sally Light which is available through the Ocean State Libraries network as well as on Amazon.com

Marian Pierre-Louis

Marian Pierre-Louis is a house historian, lecturer and writer who specializes in researching the history of New England houses. She has delivered over 100 talks at libraries, societies and conferences throughout New England and the United States on house history and genealogical topics. She is the author of the popular blog, The New England House Historian (NEHouseHistorian.blogspot. com). She maintains the Explore Historic Houses page on Facebook (https://www.facebook.com/ ExploreHistoricHouses). You can learn more about Marian and her work at www.FieldstoneHistoricResearch.com.

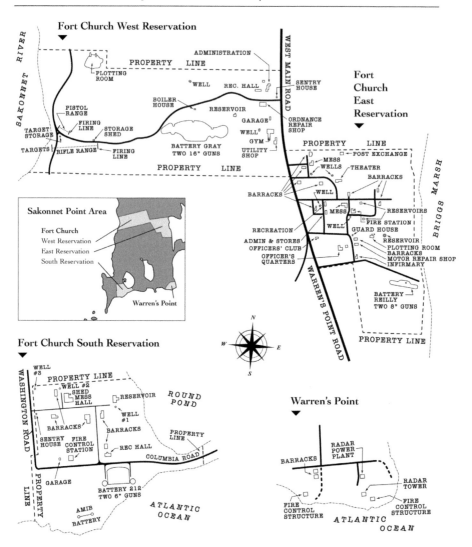

Fort Church West Reservation

▼

ADMINISTRATION
PROPERTY LINE
PLOTTING ROOM
WELL   REC. HALL
SENTRY HOUSE
BOILER HOUSE
RESERVOIR
PISTOL RANGE
GARAGE
ORDNANCE REPAIR SHOP
FIRING LINE
STORAGE SHED
WELL
GYM
TARGET STORAGE
UTILITY SHOP
TARGETS   RIFLE RANGE   FIRING LINE
BATTERY GRAY
TWO 16" GUNS
PROPERTY LINE

SAKONNET RIVER
WEST MAIN ROAD

Fort Church East Reservation

▼

PROPERTY LINE
POST EXCHANGE
MESS
WELLS   THEATER
BARRACKS
BARRACKS   WELL
RESERVOIRS
MESS
FIRE STATION
RECREATION   WELL   GUARD HOUSE
ADMIN & STORES   RESERVOIR
OFFICERS' CLUB   PLOTTING ROOM
OFFICER'S QUARTERS   BARRACKS
MOTOR REPAIR SHOP
INFIRMARY

BATTERY REILLY
TWO 8" GUNS

BRIGGS MARSH

PROPERTY LINE

WARREN'S POINT ROAD

Sakonnet Point Area

Fort Church
West Reservation
East Reservation
South Reservation

Warren's Point

N
W   E
S

Fort Church South Reservation

▼

WELL #3
PROPERTY LINE
WELL #2
SHED
MESS HALL
RESERVOIR
ROUND POND
WELL #1
BARRACKS
BARRACKS
SENTRY HOUSE   FIRE CONTROL STATION
REC HALL
PROPERTY LINE
COLUMBIA ROAD
GARAGE
BATTERY 212
TWO 6" GUNS
AMIB BATTERY
ATLANTIC OCEAN

WASHINGTON ROAD
PROPERTY LINE

Warren's Point

▼

RADAR POWER PLANT
BARRACKS
RADAR TOWER
FIRE CONTROL STRUCTURE
FIRE CONTROL STRUCTURE
ATLANTIC OCEAN

Fort Church. Map by Tom Callahan. LCHS Collection.

ENDNOTES

INTRODUCTION

1 Reverend William Emerson, *Notes on Compton, A Township in Newport County, State of Rhode-Island.* September 1803. Collections of the Massachusetts Historical Society, Vol. IX, (Boston: Munroe & Francis) 1804, p.199.

THE WILBOR HOUSE

2 There are multiple spellings of Wilbor. All come from the Wildbores (Wild Boars) of England. Today, spelling variations indicate different branches of the family. In past centuries spelling differences held less meaning. Benjamin Franklin Wilbour assigned the "Wilbor" spelling to the Wilbors in the Wilbor house, however they used a variety of spellings, most often "Wilbour" in their probate documents.

3 Carlton Brownell, *The Wilbor House*, House History Pamphlet, Undated, Little Compton Historical Society Archives, Box A24.1.

4 Restoration Slides may be viewed at: http://littlecompton.pastperfect-online.com/35259cgi/mweb.exe?request=keyword;keyword=wilbor%20house%20slide;dtype=d

5 Carlton Brownell, *The Wilbor House*, House History Pamphlet, Undated, Little Compton Historical Society Archives, Box A24.1.

6 William Wilbor's Will, 1710. Portsmouth, Rhode Island, Probate Book 2, p. 237.

7 William Wilbor On-Line Genealogy http://freepages.genealogy.rootsweb.ancestry.com/~barbpretz/ps03/ps03_192.htm

8 Carlton Brownell, *The Wilbor House*, House History Pamphlet, Undated, Little Compton Historical Society Archives, Box A24.1.

9 Carlton Brownell, *The Wilbor House*, House History Pamphlet, Undated, Little Compton Historical Society Archives, Box A24.1.

10 Will of William Wilbor the Second, 1797, Little Compton Town Council and Probate Book 3, p. 338

11 Carlton Brownell, *The Wilbor House*, House History Pamphlet, Undated, Little Compton Historical Society Archives, Box A24.1.

12 Unless otherwise noted genealogical information in this document is taken from *Little Compton Families*. Benjamin Franklin Wilbour, *Little Compton Families*, (Little Compton Historical Society: Little Compton), 1967.

13 Carlton Brownell, *The Wilbor House*, House History Pamphlet, Undated, Little Compton Historical Society Archives, Box A24.1.

14 Samuel Wilbor's Original Will & Inventory, 1740: Taunton Probate Book 9, p. 428 – 432.

15 Samuel Wilbor's Original Will & Inventory, 1740: Taunton Probate Book 9, p. 428 – 432.

16 Agreement between Samuel Wilbor's Children, 1740: Taunton Probate Book 9, p. 500-502.

17 Agreement between Samuel Wilbor's Children, 1740: Taunton Probate Book 9, p. 500-502.

18 Carlton Brownell, *The Wilbor House*, House History Pamphlet, Undated, Little Compton Historical Society Archives, Box A24.1.

19 List of Quakers in Little Compton, 1732 & 1733, *The Proprietor's Book*, Little Compton Town Vault, p. 59? (Page number obscured. Digital photograph of page in LCHS archives – Slavery-Quaker folder.)

20 Lurana Wilbor's Inventory, 1861, Little Compton, Town Council & Probate Book 11, p. 214-16.

21 Carlton Brownell, *The Wilbor House*, House History Pamphlet, Undated, Little Compton Historical Society Archives, Box A24.1.

22 Lee J. Alston and Morton Owen Schapiro, Inheritance Laws Across Colonies: Causes and Consequences, *The Journal of Economic History*, Vol. 44, No. 2, The Tasks of Economic History, (Jun., 1984), p. 277-287. Stable URL: http://www.jstor.org/stable/2120705

23 B.F. Wilbour, *Little Compton Families* p. 716.

24 Samuel Wilbor's Original Will & Inventory, 1740: Taunton Probate Book 9, p. 428 – 432. Doctor William Wilbor's Will & Inventory, 1774, Little Compton Town Council & Probate, Book 2, p. 278.

25 Little Compton Town and Vital Records, Vol. 1, May 1757.

26 Little Compton Town & Vital Records, 1758, Vol. 1, p. 76.

27 Little Compton Town & Vital Records, 1758, Vol. 1, p. 76.

28 Marjory O'Toole, *Index of Enslaved and Indentured People*, Little Compton Historical Society, 2014.

29 Carlton Brownell, *The Wilbor House*, House History Pamphlet, Undated, Little Compton Historical Society Archives, Box A24.1.

30 New York Gazette, 1774, America's Historic Newspapers

31 Kate Johnson, *Archeological Survey of the Wilbor House*, 2009. Little Compton Historical Society Archives.

32 Carlton Brownell, *The Wilbor House*, House History Pamphlet, Undated, Little Compton Historical Society Archives, Box A24.1.

33 Carlton Brownell, *The Wilbor House*, House History Pamphlet, Undated, Little Compton Historical Society Archives, Box A24.1.

34 *Little Compton Town Council and Probate*, 1774, Book 2, p. 278.

35 Lee J. Alston and Morton Owen Schapiro, Inheritance Laws Across Colonies: Causes and Consequences, *The Journal of Economic History*, Vol. 44, No. 2, The Tasks of Economic History, (Jun., 1984), p. 277-287. Stable URL: http://www.jstor.org/stable/2120705

36 Laurel Thatcher Ulrich, *A Midwife's Tale: The Life of Martha Ballard, Based on Her Diary*, 1785-1812 Vintage Books, p. 152.

37 Doctor William Wilbor, Inventory, 1774, Little Compton Town Council and Probate Book 2, p. 278-30.

38 1810 Federal Census, Little Compton, Rhode Island.

39 William Wilbor The Second, Will, Little Compton Town Council & Probate Book 3, p. 338.

40 William Wilbor, Second, Will, Little Compton Town Council & Probate Book 3, p. 338.

41 1810 Federal Census, Little Compton, Rhode Island.

42 Wilbour, *Little Compton Families*, p. 732.

43 William Wilbor The Second, Will, Little Compton Town Council & Probate Book 3, p. 338.

44 Jonathan Wilbor's Probate Records, 1822, Little Compton Town Council & Probate Book 5, p. 70 (2).

45 Jonathan Wilbor's Inventory & Priscilla Wilbor's Allowance 1822, Little Compton Town Council & Probate Book 5, p. 70-4 (2).

46 Clarke Wilbor's Will, 1823, Little Compton Town Council & Probate Book, 5 p. 77 (2).

47 Most likely two 50 acres lots, # 14 & 15, and two 11 acre lots # 5 & 4 as shown on the Proprietor's Map, LCHS Collection. The Samuel Wilbor farm was just north of the Coe farm. See page 156 for the history of the Coe farm.

48 Deborah Wilbor, Will, 1813, Little Compton Town Council & Probate Book 4, p. 444.

49 Hannah Wilbor, Will, 1825, Little Compton Town Council & Probate Book 6, p. 77.

50 Embling Wilbor Inventory, 1825, Little Compton Town Council and Probate Book 6, p. 176.

51 Hannah Wilbor, Will, 1825, Little Compton Town Council & Probate Book 6, p. 77. Embling Wilbor, Inventory, 1825, Little Compton Town Council and Probate Book 6, p. 176.

52 Lois Wilbor, Will, 1844, Little Compton Town Council and Probate Book 9, p. 204.

53 Jonathan died in debt in 1822. Jonathan Wilbor Probate Records, 1822, Little Compton Town Council and Probate Book, 5, p. 70-73(2).

54 Notes for Little Compton Historical Society Exhibit, *Learning in Little Compton*, 2014.

55 This cemetery is well known for its stone bell tower.

56 Clarke Wilbour's Will, 1855. Little Compton Town Council and Probate Book 11, p. 69-73.

57 1850 Federal Census, Little Compton, Rhode Island.

58 Janet Lisle, *The History of Little Compton: A Home by the Sea*, (Little Compton Historical Society; Little Compton, 2012) p. 236.

59 Clarke Wilbor, Will, 1856, Little Compton Town Council & Probate Book 11, p. 69-73.

60 Clarke Wilbor, Will, 1856, Little Compton Town Council & Probate Book 11, p. 69-73.

61 Lurana Wilbor's Inventory, Little Compton Town Council & Probate Book 11 p. 214-16.

62 Carlton Brownell, *The Wilbor House*, House History Pamphlet, Undated, Little Compton Historical Society Archives, Box A24.1.

63 1860 Federal Census, Little Compton, Rhode Island.

64 Lurana Wilbor's Inventory, Little Compton Town Council & Probate Book 11 p. 214-16. For information about Isaac C. Wilbor please see: *A Home by the Sea*. Janet Lisle, *The History of Little Compton: A Home by the Sea*, (Little Compton Historical Society; Little Compton, 2012)

65 David Patten, *Three Sides to the Sea*, (New York: Rinehart & Company, Inc., 1956), p. 149. Aunt Kate Wilbor was Abby Catherine Wilbor, the wife of Alexander Wilbor who lived as newlyweds in the Wilbor house in 1850.

66 This has been confirmed using Rhode Island Census records from 1865 and the 1870 Federal Census.

67 1870 Federal Census, Little Compton, Rhode Island.

68 1885 Rhode Island State Census, Little Compton.

69 1865 Rhode Island State Census, Little Compton and 1870 Federal Census, Little Compton, Rhode Island.

70 1905 Rhode Island State Census, Little Compton.

71 1875 Rhode Island State Census, Little Compton.

72 Susan Simmons Wilbor's Will, 1882, Little Compton Probate Book 12, p. 432.

73 William A. Wilbor, Will, 1886, Little Compton Town Council & Probate Book, 12, p. 630-633.

74 Oliver Wilbor Will, Little Compton Probate Book 4, p. 419-421.

75 1910 Federal Census, Little Compton, Rhode Island.

76 Oral History Interview, Catherine Fagundes Sylvia, Little Compton Historical Society, 2007.

77 Wilbor – DeAlmo Deed, May 21, 1919, Little Compton, Land Evidence Records, Book 22 p. 407.

78 Carlton Brownell, *The Wilbor House*, House History Pamphlet, Undated, Little Compton Historical Society Archives, Box A24.1.

79 Interviews with Frances Ferreira Collins, Mary O'Neil and Barbara Heywood Babbitt, 2010.

80 Miles S. Richmond report to the Little Compton Historical Society, 1954. LCHS Archive.

81 Carlton Brownell report to the Little Compton Historical Society, 1954. LCHS Archive.

82 Carlton Brownell report to the Little Compton Historical Society, 1954. LCHS Archive.

83 Carlton Brownell, *The Wilbor House*, House History Pamphlet, Undated, Little Compton Historical Society Archives, Box A24.1.

84 Little Compton Historical Society Minutes, LCHS Archive.

ONE PROPRIETOR
SIX HISTORIC HOUSES

1 Bristol County Land Evidence Records, Book 1, p. 170 & 171; Book 2, p. 237; Book 3, p. 327. Proprietor's Book, Sec. 3, p. 17.

2 Unless otherwise noted the genealogical information in the chapter is taken from: Benjamin Franklin Wilbour, *Little Compton Families*, (Little Compton Historical Society: Little Compton) 1967. For information on Nathaniel Warren see p. 698.

3 This is the southern half of the 16th 50-acre lot and the 3rd 11-acre lot. Bristol County Land Evidence Records, Book 3, p. 3.

4 Because of a change in the type of calendar used late seventeenth century early eighteenth century dates are between January and March are often listed with two years. Both are correct.

5 Bristol County Land Evidence Records, Book 3, p. 225.

6 John Bailey's will as transcribed in Wilbour, *Little Compton Families*, p. 19-20.

THE BAILEYS OF WARREN'S POINT

1 Bristol Country Probate Records, Book 10, p. 15.

2 1790 Federal Census.

3 Bristol County Probate Records, Book 10, p. 15, Bristol County Probate Records, Book 11, p. 15.

4 Little Compton Land Evidence Records, Book 1, p. 262.

5 Little Compton Land Evidence Records, Book 2, p. 201 & 295.

6 Little Compton Town Council & Probate Records, Book 2, p. 367.

7 Little Compton Land Evidence Records, Book 2, p. 201 & 295.

8 Little Compton Town Council and Probate Records, Book 2, p. 370.

9 Little Compton Land Evidence Records, Book 4, p. 326.

10 Little Compton Land Evidence Records, Book 3, pgs. 307-313, 318, 320, 322, 223, 337, 344.

11 Town Council and Probate Records, Book 4, p. 437.

12 The 1810 Federal Census shows one free person of color living in Isaac Bailey's household.

THE SEACONNET HOUSE

1   Little Compton Town Council and Probate Records, Book 8, p. 124, 130 & 30(2), 31, 37, 115.

2   The Coe family once owned the Seabury House property, please see page 156 for its house history.

3   *New-York Daily Tribune*, June 27, 1846, Image 4. Accessed via chronicling america.loc.gov/About New-York daily tribune. (New-York [N.Y.]) 1842-1866

4   Janet Lisle, *The History of Little Compton, A Home By the Sea, 1820-1950*, (Little Compton Historical Society: Little Compton), 2012, p. 88.

5   Little Compton Land Evidence Records, Book 13, p. 656.

6   Ibid., Book 12, p. 2.

7   Benjamin Franklin Wilbour, *Notes on Little Compton*, Carlton C. Brownell, ed. (Little Compton Historical Society: Little Compton), 1970, p. 71.

8   1880 Federal Census.

9   Sarah Soule Wilbor, Diary, Transcription, LCHS Archives.

10 Ancestry.com. *Washington, Passenger and Crew Lists, 1882-1961* [database on-line]. Provo, UT, USA: Ancestry.com Operations Inc., 2006.

11 Little Compton Probate Records, Book 20, p. 72.

12 Lucy O'Connor, ed., *Jonnycakes and Cream, Oral Histories of Little Compton, R.I.*, (America House Design & Communications: Newport), 1993, p. 245.

13 Ibid., p. 243.

14 Little Compton Land Evidence Records, Book 29, p. 357.

15 Interview with James Lynch, October 2014.

16 Please see Page 100 for the history of the Lunt House. Little Compton Probate Book 20, p. 148.

17 Land Evidence Book 32, p. 436.

18 Land Evidence Book 33, p. 431.

19 Interview with James Lynch, October 2014.

20 Land Evidence Book 36, p. 514.

21 Correspondence with Helen Richmond Webb, April, 2015.

THE MARSH HOUSE

1   Little Compton Land Evidence Book 8, p. 238.

2   1830 Federal Census.

3   Little Compton Land Evidence Book 11, p. 729.

4   Census records in Little Compton are challenging at this time because no street names or house numbers are listed. It is possible to infer who lived where by looking at their neighbors. This is our best interpretation of the Federal Census Records from 1830, 1850, and 1860 because Lemuel Sisson Junior appears next to families known to live on Warren's Point Road (Abraham Bailey, Henry I. Richmond and Thomas B. Grinnell). The 1840 Federal Census information is not helpful in this case because families are listed alphabetically.

5   Please see pg. 156 for the history of the Seabury House.

6   1870 Federal Census.

7   B.F. Wilbour, *Little Compton Families*, (Little Compton Historical Society: Little Compton), 1967, p. 605.

8   1860 Federal Census.

9   Little Compton Probate Book 8, p. 678 & 699.

10 Little Compton Land Evidence Book 14, p. 34.

11 Janet Lisle, *The History of Little Compton: A Home By the Sea, 1820-1950* (Little Compton Historical Society: Little Compton) 2012, p. 143.

12 See Seaconnet House History on p. 78.

13 Little Compton Land Evidence Book 20, p. 457.

14 B.F. Wilbour, *Little Compton Families,* 1967, p. 127.

15 St. Andrew's By The Sea 1914-1989, Pamphlet.

16 Little Compton Land Evidence Book 24, p. 149.

17 Little Compton Land Evidence Book 25, p. 151.

18 Little Compton Land Evidence Book 25, p. 414.

19 Little Compton Land Evidence Book 26, p. 107.

20 Family Interviews with LCHS, 2014 & 2015.

21 Family Interviews with LCHS, 2014.

22 Family Interviews with LCHS, 2014.

23 Trip Millikin Interview with LCHS, 2015.

24 Trip Millikin Interview with LCHS, 2015.

25 Family Interviews with LCHS, 2014.

THE LUNT HOUSE

1 Unless otherwise noted all genealogical information is taken from: Benjamin Franklin Wilbour, *Little Compton Families,* (Little Compton Historical Society: Little Compton), 1967. Bristol County Land Evidence Records, Book 1, p. 171. Ibid., Book 2, p. 237. Ibid., Book 3, p. 225.

2 Little Compton Town Council and Probate Records, Book 4, p. 437.

3 Ibid.

4 Biography of Henry Demarest Lloyd by Carolyn Goodrich Huntoon as quoted by: Chris Rawson, Henry Demarest Lloyd, 1846-1903, Crusading Journalist, *Portraits in Time,* (Little Compton Historical Society: Little Compton) 2008, p. 117.

5 Little Compton Land Evidence Records, Book 18, p. 478.

6 Ibid., Book 19, p. 363.

7 Ibid., Book 24, p. 475-6.

8 Caroline Strobell, *My Apple Orchard,* 1939, Little Compton Historical Society Archives, p. 1.

9 Little Compton Land Evidence Records, Book 29, p. 307.

10 Ibid., Book 34, p. 551.

11 Interview with Tom Taylor, 2014.

12 Little Compton Land Evidence Records, Book 43, p. 221.

13 Ibid., Book 232, p. 195.

14 Benjamin Franklin Wilbour, *Notes on Little Compton,* (Little Compton Historical Society: Little Compton), 1970, p. 64.

BAILEYS OF BAILEY'S LEDGE

1 Unless otherwise noted all genealogical information is taken from: Benjamin Franklin Wilbour, *Little Compton Families,* (Little Compton Historical Society: Little Compton), 1967. Bristol County Land Evidence Records, Book 3, p. 225. Ibid., Book 6, p. 276. John Bailey's Will, as transcribed in *Little Compton Families*, p. 19-20.

2 Bristol County Probate Records, Book 6, p. 374.

3 Ibid., Book 14, p. 418.

4 Marjory O'Toole, *Little Compton People of Color Database,* Little Compton Historical Society, 2014.

5 Little Compton Town Council & Probate Records, Book 2, p. 196

6 Bristol County Probate Records, Book 6, p. 374.

7 Bristol County Land Evidence Records, Book 19, p. 486.

8 Wilbour, *Little Compton Families*, p. 20.

9   Letter to Mrs. Harrison Huntoon from Glenn Irving Kientz, August 31, 1949. LCHS Archives.

10 Interview with Janet Lofsky, 2015.

11 John Bailey The Second, Will, Little Compton Town Council & Probate Book 1, p. 234.

12 Ibid.

13 1790 & 1800 Federal Censuses

14 Little Compton Town Council & Probate Records, Book 2, p. 324.

15 Ibid.

16 Little Compton Town Council & Probate Records, Book 5, p. 158.

17 Janet Lisle, *The History of Little Compton: A Home By the Sea, 1820-1950.* (Little Compton Historical Society: Little Compton) 2012, p. 35.

18 Caroline Strobell, *My Apple Orchard*, 1939, p. 2. LCHS Archives.

19 1860 Federal Census.

20 Little Compton Land Evidence Records, Book 8, p. 220 & Book 9, p. 110.

21 See page 156 for the history of the Coe family property.

22 Little Compton Land Evidence Records, Book 9, p. 110.

23 1850 Federal Census

24 Ibid.

25 Strobell, p. 2.

26 Little Compton Land Evidence Records, Book 12, p. 434.

27 Ibid., p. 326.

28 Ibid., Book 13, p. 280.

29 Ibid., Book 12, p. 654.

30 Ibid., Book 13, p. 77.

31 John Bailey, Will, Little Compton Town Council & Probate Book 11, p. 199.

32 Thankful Bailey, Will, Little Compton Town Council and Probate Book 11, p. 703.

33 Sarah Soule Wilbour, Diary, Transcription, October 4, 1890, p. 507. LCHS Archives.

34 Sarah Soule Wilbour, Diary, Transcription, December 4, 1887, p. 247. LCHS Archives.

35 Manuscript dictated by Sarah Burleigh. LCHS Archives.

36 1875 Rhode Island State Census.

37 Islands off the coast of Portugal.

38 Little Compton Federal Census, 1880.

39 Little Compton Probate Records, Book 11, p. 269.

40 Strobell, p. 2-3.

41 Little Compton Probate Records, Book 11, p. 269.

42 Letter to Mrs. Harrison Huntoon from Glenn Irving Kientz, August 31, 1949. LCHS Archives.

43 Little Compton Land Evidence Records, Book 19, p. 495.

44 Ibid., Book 21, p. 226.

45 Ibid., Book 22, p. 226.

THE HUNTOON HOUSE

1   Lucy O'Connor, ed. *Jonnycakes and Cream, Oral Histories of Little Compton, R.I.,* (American House Design & Communications, Newport) 1993, p. 80.

2   Little Compton Land Evidence Records Book 22, p. 322.

3   Jeanette Huntoon believed that the house was built in 1710. Evidence in local histories, historic maps, and in the architecture of the house suggests that the original Bailey homestead (c. 1707) was located in "The Orchard" to the northwest of the Huntoon House.

4   Little Compton Land Evidence Records, Book 23, p. 100 & 380.

5   Letter to Mrs. Harrison Huntoon from Glenn Irving Kientz, August 31, 1949. LCHS Archives.

THE STROBELL-GOODRICH COTTAGE

1 Little Compton Land Evidence Records, Book 21, p.226.

2 Little Compton Land Evidence Records, Book 21, p.363-364.

3 Chris Rawson, *Where Stonewalls Meet the Sea*, Sakonnet Golf Club, Limited Edition 1999, p. 74, Interview in 1982 of Lloyd Goodrich.

4 Little Compton Land Evidence Records, Book 22, p. 226.

5 Chris Rawson, Ibid., p.78.

6 David L. Goodrich, *My Well-Spent Youth*, Beckham Publications Group, 2009, p.55.

7 Caroline Strobell, *My Apple Orchard*, 1939, Little Compton Historical Society Archives.

8 Madeleine Goodrich Noble, email to Claudia Bell, April 1, 2015.

9 David L.Goodrich, *The Real Nick and Nora*, Southern University Press, 2001, p.8.

10 Madeleine Goodrich Noble, email to Claudia Bell, April 24, 2015.

11 www.digicoll.library.wisc.edu/cgi/f/findaid, Henry Demarest Lloyd Papers.

12 David L. Goodrich, *My Well-Spent Youth*, p.55.

13 Ibid., p.55.

14 David L. Goodrich, *The Real Nick and Nora*, p.56.

15 David L. Goodrich, *My Well-Spent Youth*, p.57.

16 Telephone Interview of Phil Havens by Claudia Bell, April 5, 2015. Email from Madeleine Noble Goodrich to Claudia Bell, April 1, 2015.

17 Little Compton Land Evidence Records, Book 28, p.298.

18 Email from Madeleine Noble Goodrich to Claudia Bell, April 1, 2015.

19 Little Compton Town Evidence Records, Book 29, p. 43.

20 Chris Rawson, *Where Stonewalls Meet the Sea*, Excerpt from 1982 Lloyd Goodrich Interview, p. 77.

21 David L. Goodrich, *My Well-Spent Youth*, p.65.

22 Email from Frannie Hall to Little Compton Historical Society, April 29, 2015.

23 Email from Madeleine Noble to Claudia Bell, April 30, 2015.

24 Ibid.

25 David L. Goodrich, *The Real Nick and Nora*, p.8.

26 David L. Goodrich, *My Well-Spent Youth*, p. 67.

27 David L. Goodrich, *The Real Nick and Nora*, p.56.

28 Interview of Janet Lofsky by Marjory O'Toole, April 2015.

29 *New York Times* obituary of Lloyd Goodrich, March 28, 1987.

30 Telephone interview of Phil Havens by Claudia Bell, April 5, 2015.

31 Email from Phil Havens to Claudia Bell, March 30, 2015 and telephone interview April 5, 2015.

32 Email from Madeleine Goodrich Noble to Claudia Bell, April 25, 2015.

33 Email from Frannie Hall to the Little Compton Historical Society, April 29, 2015.

34 David L. Goodrich, *My Well-Spent Youth*, p.59, and telephone interview with Phil Havens, April 5, 2015.

35 Ibid., p.60

36 Ibid., p.61.

37 Little Compton Land Evidence Records, Book 32, p.210.

38 Little Compton Land Evidence Records, Book 69, p.115.

39 Chris Rawson, *Where Stonewalls Meet the Sea*, p. 187.

THE SEABURY HOUSE

1   The Proprietor's Book, First Part, May 21, 1775, p. 5.
2   Bristol County Land Evidence Records, Book 3, p. 3.
3   Unless otherwise noted all genealogical information is taken from: Benjamin Franklin Wilbour, *Little Compton Families*, (Little Compton Historical Society: Little Compton) 1967.
4   Bristol County Land Evidence Records, Book 3, p. 4.
5   Ibid., Book 3, p. 5.
6   Ibid., Book 6, p. 198
7   Little Compton Town Council and Probate Records, Book 2, p. 431.
8   Janet Lisle, *The History of Little Compton: First Light Sakonnet, 1660-1820*, (Little Compton Historical Society: Little Compton), 2010, p. 125.
9   See page 68 for the history of the Baileys of Warren's Point.
10 Little Compton Town Council & Probate Records, Book 5, p. 97.
11 Little Compton Land Evidence Records, Book 7, p. 91.
12 Ibid., Book 9, p. 157.
13 Ibid., Book 10, p. 158.
14 Ibid., Book 12, p. 303.
15 Ibid., Book 12, p. 303.
16 Wilbour, p. 606.
17 Wilbour, p. 544.
18 Little Compton Land Evidence Records, Book 12, p. 645.
19 Ibid., Book 14, p. 79.
20 *Historic and Architectural Resources of Little Compton, RI*; Rhode Island Historical Preservation Commission, 1990, p. 83.
21 Little Compton Land Evidence Records, Book 15, p. 275.
22 Little Compton Probate Records, Book 15, p. 442-445, & 462.
23 Interview with former employee. April 29, 2015.

THE HEAD HOUSE

1   Little Compton Proprietors' Book, Section 1, p. 3. Located in the Little Compton Town Hall Vault.
2   Bristol County Land Evidence Records, Book 6, p. 374. Ibid., Book 8, p. 258. Ibid., Book 9, p. 661.
3   Little Compton Proprietors' Book, Section 1, p. 14.
4   Bristol Country Probate Records, Book 3, p. 286.
5   Little Compton Town Council and Probate Records, Book 1, p. 166.
6   Ibid., p. 164.
7   Ibid., p. 294(2).
8   Ibid., Book 3, p. 323. Ibid., pg. 467
9   Ibid., p. 471.
10 Little Compton Land Evidence Records, Book 3 p. 474.
11 Ibid., p. 514
12 Ibid., p. 91. Little Compton Town Council and Probate Records, Book 3, p. 323. Ibid., p. 514
13 Little Compton Land Evidence Records, Book 3 pg. 562
14 Ibid., p. 156
15 For more information on this property which later included the Albert T. Sisson House please see p. 156. Little Compton Land Evidence Records, Book 12, p. 303.
16 Not to be confused with Seaconnet House at the corner of West Main and Warren's Point Roads which was owned by the Richmonds at this time. Please see page 78 for the Seaconnet House.
17 Interview with Avis Buxton Child, 2012.
18 Interviews with Donald Truchon, 2012 & 2014.
19 Please see page 88 for the Marsh House.
20 Interview with Elizabeth (Bunny) Philippi Millikin, May 19, 2015.

21 Interview with Avila Moore, May 19, 2015.

22 Interviews with Richard Bixby, 2012 & 2014.

23 Little Compton Land Evidence Records, Book 76, p. 55.

THE NUMBER 4 SCHOOL HOUSE

1 Unless otherwise noted all genealogical information is taken from: Benjamin Franklin Wilbour, *Little Compton Families*, (Little Compton Historical Society: Little Compton), 1967. See Tobias Brown's will, p. 73.

2 Little Compton Town Council and Probate Records, Book 3, p. 221.

3 Ibid., Book 5, p. 9(2).

4 Ibid., Book 5, p. 16(2) & 371. Ibid., Book 6, p. 284, 286, 289 & 291.

5 Ibid., Book 5, p. 373.

6 Little Compton Land Evidence Records, Book 5, p. 676.

7 Little Compton Town Council and Probate Records, Book 6, p. 311(2).

8 Ibid., Book 9, p. 219. Little Compton Land Evidence Records, Book 8, p. 115.

9 Little Compton Town Council and Probate Records, 116(2), 191, 312(2).

10 Little Compton Land Evidence Records, Book 10, p. 52.

11 Thomas McCarthy, Unpublished manuscript. LCHS Archives.

12 A replica of Peaked Top School is on display at the Little Compton Historical Society. For more on schools in Little Compton please see: Janet Lisle, *The History of Little Compton: A Home By the Sea, 1820-1950*, (Little Compton Historical Society: Little Compton), 2012.

13 Little Compton Land Evidence Records, Book 16, p. 379. Please see p. 100 for the history of the Peleg Bailey Farm and the Lunt House.

14 Number 4 Schoolhouse Registers 1903-1927. LCHS Archives.

15 *Annual Report of the Superintendent of Public Schools in the Town of Little Compton, RI, for the year ending April 30, 1885.* LCHS Archives.

16 Ibid., p. 8.

17 Some of the lumber from the schoolhouse was used to build Manuel Fagundes' garage on West Main Road according to his daughter, Catherine Fagundes Silvia.

18 1891-92 Annual Report of the School Committee of the Town of Little Compton, RI, Also the Reports of Superintendent of Schools, p. 3 & 6. LCHS Archives.

19 Ibid., p. 12.

20 Annual Report of the Superintendent of Public Schools in the Town of Little Compton, RI, for the year ending April 30, 1899. p. 7. LCHS Archives.

21 Ibid., for the year ending April 30, 1901 p. 6.

22 Ibid., for the year ending April 30, 1905, p. 4.

23 Ibid., for the year ending March 31, 1907 Pgs. 3-4.

24 Ibid., for the year ending March 31, 1909 Pgs. 3-4.

25 Ibid., for the year ending March 31, 1912, Pg. 3.

26 Ibid., for the year ending June 30, 1914 Pg. 16. Ibid., for the year ending June 30, 1916 p. 16. Ibid., for the year ending June 30, 1919 Pg. 17. Ibid., for the year ending June 30, 1920 Pg. 17.

27 Interview with Virginia Watt, 2013.

28 1924 State School Report R.I. Public Education Service Report of Committee on Survey of Little Compton Public Schools Supplementary Report of the State Board of Education 1924 p. 8 & 18.

29 Little Compton Land Evidence Records, Book 26, p. 112.

30 Interview with Barbara Camara Passmore, May 15, 2015. 1940 Federal Census.

31 Little Compton Land Evidence Records, Book 33, p. 80.

32 Ibid., Book 36, p. 331.

33 Ibid., Book 53, p. 403. Ibid., Book 108, p. 1. Ibid., Book 156, p. 649.

William and Susan Wilbor were among the last Wilbors to live in the Wilbor House.
B.F. Wilbour Scrapbook. LCHS Collection.

Seaconnet House, c. 1958. Courtesy of William Richmond.

INDEX